SPHERE COLOUR PLANT GUIDES
TREES AND SHRUBS

SPHERE BOOKS LIMITED
30-32 Gray's Inn Road, London WCIX 8JL

CONTENTS

Production: Inmerc BV, Wormer, Holland, and Mercurius Horticultural Printers, 11 East Stockwell Street, Colchester, Essex.
Compilation: Rob van Maanen.
Text: Michiel Dronkers, Rob van Maanen.
Translation: Sue Baker.
Photography: Joop Valk, Paul Kuiper, Bob van der Lans, Proefstation voor de Fruitteelt te Wilhelminadorp.
Photo cover: Hannes Rosenberg.
Layout: Loek de Leeuw.
Typesetting: RCO/Telezet BV, Velp.
Printing: BV Kunstdrukkerij Mercurius-Wormerveer, Holland.
This edition published by Sphere Books Ltd, London 1983.
© 1983 Mercbook International Ltd., Guernsey.

INTRODUCTION

Trees in the landscape

Trees are indispensable. A world without trees is a lost world. This is not only because a treeless landscape looks deserted and inhospitable, but also because trees – amongst other things – are the greatest providers of oxygen, without which life on earth is insupportable. It is virtually impossible to overrate the importance of trees, particularly in our heavily populated country. So it is not surprising that a gradual awareness has grown that trees are more important than expansion plans for industry and government.

Trees have another function. They 'dress the landscape'. Imagine the desert with its bare, rocky terrain or pure sand; and compare this with a green forest where trees and plants fight for space. Can you imagine people and animals in the desert? And in the forest? Even if neither of them holds an immediate appeal, if you had to choose you would pick the forest because you would find life there.

Part of the Sahara was also green not so long ago, but this disappeared over a couple of centuries because the use of the plants and trees was too intensive. The same could happen to the greatest of our still living forests: the rain forests of the Amazon, known as the 'lung of the world'. If the reckless cutting of this wood continues, life on earth will gradually deteriorate. Such changes happen so slowly that we only notice them by the disappearance of some animals and plants. But the loss of a forest is irreversible because the fertile topsoil is washed and blown away if the trees no longer hold it in place. Every time we plant a tree we are holding back this process. Because of this, many countries now have a 'plant a tree day' when everyone plants a tree: everyone, that is, who realises the impossibility of having a fertile country without them.

And we have not yet mentioned the protection from sun or pouring rain that is offered by a tree!

Beside the kingly tree, the shrub is but a knight, a lowly subject. However, the advantage of the shrub is that its branches begin low on the ground and it offers protection as a hedge which can be impenetrable. In addition, there are shrubs with the most beautifully coloured flowers and fruit.

Actually, shrubs are either small trees or large plants. As plants, they need so much space that they are unsuitable for a small garden, but as trees they are small enough for a slightly larger garden. That is why we often see them in parks and public gardens, which in size rank somewhere between a wood and a private garden. Heather, which is also a shrub because of its woody stem,

usually only grows about 30 cm tall. So the diversity of trees and shrubs is immense.

May be you will say that it is all very well to learn more about trees and shrubs but what can you do with them? Your garden is not large enough for a chestnut tree that grows to 20 metres with a crown of about the same size. Then you will be pleased to know that heather is not the only small shrub. Did you know that the rose is a shrub; that there are shrubs with berries that grow no higher than half a metre; and that there are even trees that reach no more than this height? Everyone with a garden will find something suitable in this guide, but if you have the room...

There is a saying that goes: 'each of us has three tasks to fulfil in life – to produce an heir, to write a book and to plant a tree; only then can we die in peace'.

Well, planting a tree is simple enough, so what are you waiting for?

Classification

With a few exceptions, trees and shrubs belong to the larger plants. From a botanical point of view a tree is 'a woody, perennial plant, that can be decades or centuries old, and bears flowers and fruit annually'.

The same goes for a shrub, but the difference is that a tree has a trunk on which the branches form at a certain level above the ground, whilst the branches of the shrub begin immediately at ground level. It is this difference that has determined the classification used for the plants in this guide.

But apart from this main division, there are also subdivisions that will tell you more about trees and shrubs.

To start with, the trees are sub-divided into those with leaves – the foliates – and those with needles – the conifers. The leaves of the foliates differ considerably and these trees are almost always deciduous. They also have wide crowns of thick branches. In general, their wood is harder than that of the conifers. Well known foliates common in this country include oak, beech, birch, willow and chestnut. The conifers are mostly evergreens with straight trunks and small, thin branches. Most of them grow quickly and the wood is easy to use because of its straight grain: this is why most woods planted for the furniture or paper industries are of conifers. As a group, they tend to be more interesting for the gardener because there are more low growing varieties than there are of the foliates. But all the most well known of both groups will be found in this guide.

Most attention, though, is given to the shrubs. This very important group of garden plants is firstly classified as deciduous or evergreen. The evergreen shrubs generally have a fairly thick, leathery leaf, whilst that of the deciduous shrubs looks more like the leaf of the foliate. Then the shrubs are often divided by how much they bloom. In fact, all shrubs flower, but with some this is hardly noticeable, whilst for others (e.g. the rose and azalea) it is spectacular. Because of this, shrubs are often said to be either flowering or non-flowering. There is also a division to be made in the way in which they bloom: they do this either on the old or the new wood. 'On the old wood' means that the buds have already formed before the winter; 'on the new wood' that buds form on the new shoots that develop in spring. So, the early blooming shrubs flower on the old wood and the late bloomers on the new. And it is important to know whether a shrub blooms early or late in order to prune it correctly and at the right time. This subject is covered at the end of the introduction.

To sum up, the most important classifications for trees and shrubs are: foliates and conifers, deciduous and evergreen, flowering or non-flowering, early and late bloomers.

With very few exceptions, all trees and shrubs bear fruit, and in some cases this is edible. A seperate section of this guide is devoted to fruit trees and shrubs, covering the most

common, e.g. apples, pears, berries and grapes. With some of these trees and shrubs the fruit itself is very pretty and others have lovely blossom, and these look nice when mixed with other decorative plants. However, fruit trees generally need more care and that is why they have their own chapter.

For a similar reason, the final main section concerns hedges. Obviously, a hedge is not a separate type of plant, but anything used for this purpose needs slightly different instructions, particularly for planting and pruning.

The chapter headings in this guide therefore correspond with these main classifications for trees and shrubs.

About soil, light and moisture

You may have been able to form some idea of the types of trees and shrubs you would like in your garden from the classifications.

To help you make a sensible choice – one which allows for

the situation in your garden – we must look at what each plant needs from its surroundings. First of all there is the soil in which the plants stand, and which supplies food, water and oxygen. If you want to plant shrubs or conifers in your garden, the earth must be heavy enough to hold the roots firmly; only then will the plant remain upright during a storm. Besides this function, the earth also provides the goodness needed by a plant. The plant takes food from the soil through the threadlike ends of the roots. To transport this food, water is necessary, which the plant also takes from the earth. In addition, moisture is necessary to keep the plant cool in hot weather. Finally, the earth plant with oxygen so that the roots can breath.

The soil is therefore of vital importance for the plant in several ways.

One type of soil answers the demands of a plant better than another, and you will need to know if the earth in your garden is good enough to successfully sow or plant. So here is some information about the different types of soil and their good and bad points.

The most common in Britain are: clay, peat, sand and loam. Of the clay soils, the river – and young sea – clays give the best drainage; i.e. they are the most crumbly. Water and oxygen can circulate freely. These clays are very suitable for the garden, although they must be well fertilised in order to give the plant sufficient food. The other types of clayey earth are too badly drained and too fat to be used as garden soil.

Peat forms a very good soil when lime, sand and manure are added. But this generally very wet soil needs extra attention to drainage.

Sandy soil is usually well drained and rich in lime but poor in goodness; mix with compost or stable manure and in summer fertilise regularly since it does not hold its goodness.

Water well, too, because moisture quickly drains away. Finally, loam is a granular soil that contains some clay.

The more clay, the harder it is to work, but most loam in this country is fairly light and contains sufficient goodness. The ideal garden soil is crumbly and loose and contains a varied assortment of foods.

In addition the ingredients of soil, air and water are present in more or less equal quantities. No one soil matches this ideal, but every soil can be improved. In most cases you can do this by regularly digging in organic fertiliser; i.e. peat, compost (leaf mould) and stable manure.

But if you want to tackle the improvement of your garden soil more throughly, you can have a soil analysis done by specialists. On the basis of this analysis, they will tell you

precisely what you need to do to improve your soil.

In the explanatory text in this guide we give, where necessary, the type of earth best suited to a plant. If this is not specified, the plant will grow in just about any good earth. A plant does not, however, live just from the soil. For growth and flowering light is needed; light provides the energy which develops the plant. And although this energy is generally necessary for the growth of a plant, there are many plants that will grow in shade but only flower in full sun.

So you must bear this in mind when planting out your garden. There are, it is true, some plants that flower in shade, but most, particularly those from seed, only flower with at least two hours of sun per day. Where a plant has a definite preference for sun or shade, you will find this in the text.

If soil and sun are important considerations when choosing where to plant, then so is moisture. If you live on low ground, the soil will generally be damper; peat is often soggy, so good drainage is necessary to ensure the plants survive.

On the other hand, we have established that sandy soil with its crumbly structure does not hold water: even in lowlying areas, the ground can be just 10 cm above water level and still be dry. So with sandy soil regular watering is imperative to keep your plants alive. For peat and for sand, the advice is the same: mix the earth with leaf mould and, respectively, sand or peat mould in order to create a consistency that gives good drainage or water retention. Alternatively, you can also select your plants according to soil type. If the earth is sandy you can choose, for example, a rock or heather garden. If you live on damp ground, then consider a garden of reeds and water plants. In most cases, though, and certainly if you live in a town, the situation is not this extreme and you can, with some thought, create a garden in which the different varieties of plants all feel at home.

Instructions

A plant makes demands on soil and climate, but it also needs looking after. Although a fruit tree needs a lot more care than an elm, the following will give you a general idea of how to plant and prune trees and shrubs. In addition, at the beginning of each chapter you will also find more specific information on the care of that particular group.

When to plant

These days most trees and shrubs are sold in soluble pots; you put plant and pot into the ground. The advantage is that you are no longer restricted to a particular season for planting. However, if you buy a plant with bare roots or in a non-soluble container, then the following rules will be of assistance:

– plant deciduous shrubs and trees during their leafless period; i.e. between late October and late March, but avoid snowy or frosty days.

– evergreens should be planted late summer (between August and October) or in spring.

If you keep to these rules, there is little that can go wrong.

Planting

Before planting a tree or shrub, make sure the earth is well dug so that the plant can establish itself easily.

Dig a hole of about half a metre deep by the same width (for young plants; older plants will obviously need more room). Mix the soil with compost, sand or peat: sand for lime loving plants, and peat for those that like acid soil. Usually trees and shrubs do not have a particular preference, but if they do you will find this in the text.

Before you put the young tree or shrub into the hole, saturate its roots by standing it in a bucket of water for a quarter of an hour. Also, pour several buckets of water into the hole itself.

The tree or shrub can now be planted to the same depth as

previously – you can see this from the stem. Fill in the hole with earth and pack down (not too tightly) and finally put a layer of manure around the stem.

For taller trees and shrubs, keep an area of at least 2 metres free around the stem. With shorter plants this space can be a bit less. But in general the more room you give a tree or shrub, the better its development.

Transplanting

The rules on when to plant also apply to transplanting trees and shrubs. You must be very careful when lifting the plant. It is inevitable that the roots will suffer some damage, but this can be limited by remembering that the roots spread to the same width as the branches. Even when it is impossible to work the plant loose to such a width (and depth!), you should lift as much of the root as possible, because if the plant loses too much of its roots it can no longer get enough moisture and will dry out. From this,

you will have deduced that it is better to leave the transplanting of large trees to the experts.

Once lifted, the same rules apply as for planting.

Pruning

In general, trees and shrubs should be pruned to keep them in shape, literally and figuratively. It influences the growth and bloom of the plant. Pruning can keep a shrub low and thick, can prevent bare patches and provide a stronger growth. The more a plant is pruned, the stronger it becomes; but with young trees and shrubs it can also mean that they lose a lot of their bud bearing wood. It is therefore important, particularly with fruit trees and flowering shrubs, to prune just the right amount. There is more information on pruning in the short introductions to the main chapters. For foliates, conifers and hedges, pruning is mainly done to keep the plant in shape, to remove dead branches and to avoid bare patches. If you lop off one of the larger branches, treat the scar with tar or a specially developed lotion.

To work!

Now that you know a bit more about the varieties and the care they need, you can make good use of the information on the following pages. Leaf through the guide and gain some ideas on how to give your garden a different appearance.

Obviously, the information in this guide is limited, but once you have made a choice you can discuss it with your nurseryman. He will happily give you the benefit of his expertise. For that reason we have chosen to illustate as wide a selection of plants as possible. This means that from many widely known plants just the main varieties are included, while in fact there may be many different types of this one plant. For example, the guide is not meart to provide information about every type of azalea, but about as many different shrubs as possible. In this way, the guide covers the main varieties which are applicable in our climate and available in most gardencentres.

The plants in each chapter were arranged in alphabetical order of the Latin names, because you will find that these names are used in most nurseries and gardencentres. If however you want to look up a plant but do not know its Latin name, you will find the English name and the according page(s) in the general index – in which both Latin and English names appear. Obviously, the information in this guide is limited, but once you have made a choice you can discuss it with your nurseryman. He will happily give you the benefit of his expertise. We wish you many pleasant hours in your garden!

CHAPTER 1

SHRUBS

As you have discovered from the introduction, there are large and small, flowering and non-flowering, deciduous and evergreen shrubs. It is worth studying this huge variety because it is shrubs in particular that give your garden its atmosphere.

Together with the trees, they decide the general picture of the garden and form a background for the garden plants. A wall of shrubs creates atmosphere by the protection it affords, and its shape and colour can form an harmonious whole with the other plants in your garden. To achieve a happy combination, it is necessarry to give some careful thought to the selection of shrubs. Because, no matter how pretty a shrub is, if it does not mix with the plants around it, it can mar the total look of the garden.

Colourful shrubs work well in combination with a green or restful background, but they jar the eyesight if planted amongst other equally as colourful plants. Of course, this is not a hard and fast rule, but it is sensible to mix and match the colours of your plants carefully. In most cases a garden is built up of evergreen shrubs or conifers (for fencing and padding) and several groups of colourful flowers; flowering shrubs and/or garden plants. On page 11 there is a picture of another idea: through the use of shrubs the garden has become a sort of cave. A heather garden is another example of the use of shrubs. So there are plenty of possibilities with shrubs. Information about planting and care can be found in the general introduction, to which can be added:

– shrubs that bloom on the young wood can be well pruned in winter or early spring.

– shrubs that bloom on the old wood should be lightly pruned immediately after they have flowered.

Where these instructions and those in the general introduction apply to the shrubs described in this chapter, you will find no further mention in the text under the photos.

ACER palmatum 'Atropurpureum'
Maple (Japanese)

Flowering period: June.
Colour: purple-red(flowers), green(summer leaf), dark red(autumn leaf).
Height: 3 metres, and about the same in width.
The Japanese maple is an extremely attractive shrub that loses its leaves after they have turned to a deep red in the autumn (see cover photo which shows an acer palmatum). The maple should be planted preferably in acid ground in a well protected spot, free standing in a border, rock or roof garden. The Japanese maple does not like dryness but copes reasonably well with frost and a city atmosphere.

ACER palmatum 'Dissectum Atropurpureum'
Maple (Japanese)

Flowering period: insignificant.
Colour: green(summer leaf), russet(autumn leaf).
Height: 1.5 m tall, 2-3 m wide.
This is another maple which looks decorative in the garden. Because it is not very tall, there are many possibilities for combining it with other shrubs or plants. It needs acid soil and a sheltered spot. Unlike the A. palm. 'Atropurpureum', this maple is completely winter resistant and copes quite well with dryness.
Otherwise, the 'ordinary' maples, which are in the main trees, are generally stronger than the cultivated ones. Maples shed their leaves.

AESCULUS carnea
Red Horse Chestnut

Flowering period: June.
Colour: pale red or flesh coloured(flowers).
Height: 15-20 metres.
This is not a pure horse chestnut but a hybrid raised in the previous century by crossing A. pavia and A. hippocastanum, the white horse chestnut. The rather large, hand shaped leaves, which form at the end of long stems, are dark green in colour, changing to yellow in the autumn. The tree likes a sunny spot and moist, but well drained, soil. It looks nicer if it is not pruned. A disadvantage is that very little can grow underneath its tight crown.

AMELANCHIER lamarckii
Snowy Mespilus

Flowering period: April to May.
Colour: white(blossom), green(summer leaf), orange-red(autumn leaf), purple(fruit).
Height: 3-5 metres, and the same in width.
The Amelanchier, which comes from Nort America, makes few demands as far as soil, sun and moisture are concerned. In the spring it is a mass of blossom; in the autumn it is covered in orange-red leaves. Because of its very bushy growth it is better to plant it on its own. It is very sturdy and does not mind a city atmosphere. The blossom attracts bees and the fruit is edible.

AMPELOPSIS veitchii
Vine

Flowering period: insignificant.
Colour: shiny green(leaf).
Height: 8-15 metres.
The vine, although a climber, does not have such a stranglehold as the knotgrass and therefore poses no danger to the trees in your garden. In autumn the leaf, which is pointed with three segments, turns wine red. A lovely plant with which to cover a high wall, even one that faces north. And it needs no assistance because its suckers give it a good grip. But do not allow it to grow around wooden window frames or over roofs.

AZALEA japonica
Japanese Azalea

Flowering period: April to May.
Colour: red, lilac, pink, white, orange, blue.
Height: 60-120 cm.
Some Japanese azaleas lose their leaves but just as many other varieties remain green. This shrub should be planted in acid, moist soil in a sheltered spot – particularly away from north and east winds. This type of azalea will grow in both sun and partial shade, but it does not like dryness. The soil should be kept acid: to this end treat regularly with peat mould, but not too near the plant – the roots lie quite close to the surface. Protect young plants from frost.

AZALEA knaphill-exbury
Azalea

Flowering period: late May to June.
Colour: white, yellow, pink, orange, red.
Height: up to 150 cm tall, to 2 m wide.
The knaphill-exbury azaleas are stronger than the Japanese variety. They bloom later than most other azaleas but, like the others, they need moist, acid soil in a well sheltered spot in partial shade. Propagation takes place from cuttings. Regular treatment with peat mould will keep the soil acid – peat mould is not only acid but it also holds water which keept the roots nice and damp. The knaphill-exbury azalea usually has fragrant flowers.

AZALEA mollis
Azalea

Flowering period: May.
Colour: pink, red, orange, yellow.
Height: 100-200 cm.
These azaleas, too, need acid, moist soil and a sheltered spot in sun or partial shade. In general azaleas do not need to be pruned, but if this becomes necessary it should be done in April.
Full blown flowers should be cut off in order to encourage as many blooms as possible. The deciduous mollis has beautiful tinted leaves in autumn. It is fairly winter resistant; but when crossed with the less sturdy sinensis some protection against frost is necessary.

AZÁLEA
Azalea

From a botanical point of view the name azalea is incorrect because all the varieties belong to the extensive rhododendron family which consists of two groups: 1. Eurhodendron, which very seldom sheds its leaves; 2. Anthodendron, which as a rule does lose its leaves in winter. This latter group is commonly known as the azalea. Even more confusing (for those who know Greek) is that the word azalea comes from the Greek *azaleos* which means dry, but in fact the plant needs a cool, rather shady and damp spot. We are only talking about garden varieties here and not pot plants like the Azalea indica. Rhododendrons, and therefore azaleas, should be planted in moist, well drained, fertile and lime free soil. Before planting, they should soak for two hours in lime free (rain) water. Make sure the root clump is slightly below the surface because after planting the ground tends to subside a bit. If the ground is not already peaty, leaf mould or peat litter must be added. Treat with old manure at the beginning of winter, and before the plant flowers, in March-April, give it a dose of liquid fertiliser and superphosphate, 3 kg to 100 litres of water. If possible, it is a good idea to mix the soil with earth in which azaleas or rhododendrons have already grown, because this contains a beneficial mould. Azalea roots lie very close to the surface of the soil so it is better not to dig the ground around permanent plants. Fallen leaves should be left as they make good insulation and feed the plant once they have rotted. For the same reason, it is also a good idea to put grass cuttings, wet turf or a layer of rotted leaves around the plant. In general azaleas do not need to be pruned, but if this must be done then it should be in April. Full blown flowers, however, must be cut off, otherwise the plant will use too much energy in forming seed. This detracts from the plant's appearance and also means that fewer flowers will form. Azaleas can be planted at about one metre intervals, preferably in light shade, although some garden hybrids will do well in full sun providing they get sufficient moisture. A short description of the main groups:1. Azalea mollis (hybrids). The most common type, also known as the garden azalea. It can grow to a height of 2 metres and flowers mid-May. 'Polly' Claessens', bright red. 'Salmon Queen', yellow-orange. 'Adrian Koster', yellow. 'William Strong-iron', orange-red. 'Radiant', dark red. 'Susanna Loef', deep pink.
2. Azalea occidentalis (hybrids). These look like the azaleas from the previous group, but they bloom a little later and have much brighter coloured flowers. 'Pink Cloud', pink. 'Magnifica', creamy yellow with orange flecks. 'Exquisita', pale pink with yellow-orange flecks.
3. Knaphill and Exbury azaleas. A group of English hybrids, with large, wide open flowers. 'Satan', red. 'Klondyke', golden yellow. 'Cecile', pink with a yellow fleck. 'Persil', pure white with a yellow fleck.
4. Japanese azaleas. These are the only azaleas that keep their leaves, either completely or partly. They are also the only ones that do well in full sun, as long as the soil is damp. This group contains small flowered variaties that grow no higher than 50 cm, and others with large flowers that reach about 100 cm. Those with small flowers include 'Adonis', white. 'Amoena', lilac to purple. 'Blauws Pink', pink. Among the larger varieties are 'Palestrina', white. 'Favorite', pink. 'Orange Beauty', orange. 'Christina', red. 'Lilac Time', lilac.

BERBERIS frikartii 'Amstelveen'
Barberry

Flowering period: May to June.
Colour: yellow(flower), green(leaf).
Height: 50-80 cm.
The cultivated berberis 'Amstelveen' is an evergreen shrub found in many parks because it is particularly sturdy. It needs a somewhat acid soil but otherwise makes few demands on the soil or the surroundings – it grows just as well in the town or along the roadside as it does in the wild. Because of the dense foliage, this shrub is also used for hedges. It can be propagated in the summer from cuttings.

BERBERIS linearifolia 'Orange King'
Barberry

Flowering period: May to June.
Colour: yellow-orange(flower), dark green(leaf).
Height: 80-120 cm.
This one comes from Chile and is armed with sharp thorns. Not surprisingly for a South American plant, it copes better with dryness than with frost. After it has flowered, blue berries appear so the plant continues to look attractive.
With al little care and some fertiliser, it will flower a second time in the autumn. It keeps its leaves and is propagated by seed. It can be planted on its own or in small groups, and with its sharp thorns it makes an impenetrable hedge.

BERBERIS thunbergii 'Atropurpurea'
Barberry

Flowering period: insignificant.
Colour: yellow(flower), red(berry), green(summer leaf), dark red(autumn leaf).
Height: 1 to 1.5 m.
The berberis thunbergii was discovered in 1784 in Japan by Thunberg. It is a deciduous shrub that makes no special demands on the soil and is very winter resistant. Because of the dense growth this berberis, too, is often used as a hedge – although in winter it is rather bald.
Other possibilities are: planted alone or in small groups, in the border, rock or heather garden. Propagation from seed in April.

BERBERIS thunbergii 'Atropurpurea Nana'
Barberry

Flowering period: insignificant.
Colour: red(berry), green(summer leaf), brown(autumn leaf).
Height: 30 cm.
This dwarf berberis is a smaller version of the previously described Berberis thunb. 'Atropurpurea'. Because of its small, ball-shaped growth it is particularly suitable, either alone or in groups, for rock garden or border. Otherwise, the directions for the previous Berberis apply to this one.

BUDDLEIA davidii
Buddleia

Flowering period: July to September.
Colour: violet(flowers).
Height: 200-250 cm.
This shrub, which comes from West China, is well known for the remarkable number of butterflies which it attracts during the summer. The leaves are dark green and grow opposite each other. Because the flowers only form along the one year old wood, it must be cut back in early spring to a height of 30 cm. It grows in any fairly fertile garden soil in a sunny, protected spot, but it must have sufficient space in which to spread itself.

CALLICARPA bodinieri 'Profusion'
Beauty Berry

Flowering period: July to August.
Colour: pink(flowers), purple(berries).
Height: 150 cm.
This is a rather rare decorative shrub that is very suitable for smaller gardens. Its flowers are not particularly remarkable, but the beautiful purple berries which appear in September make it very decorative. It has tapering, oval leaves, 6-12 cm in length. At the top of the branches these are slightly brown in colour, but elsewhere they are dull green. Because these trees cross-pollinate, it is recommended that several are planted together.

CAMPSIS radicans
Trumpet Vine

Flowering period: August to September.
Colour: red-orange(flowers).
Height: 12 metres.
This is a very sturdy climbing shrub that comes from the forests of America. It is a fast grower, and its branches are covered in what looks like fine hairs. It has strong roots, but even so it is a good idea to give it extra support against a wall. The feathery leaf consists of 9-11 small coarse veined leaves which measure 3-6 cm. Its flowers, 6-9 cm long, are trumpet shaped. It must have fertile soil, is winter resistant, and in late February must be pruned back.

CAMPSIS tagliabuana 'Mme Galen'
Trumpet Vine

Flowering period: August to September.
Colour: orange-red(flower).
Height: up to 6 metres(climber).
The Campsis tagliabuana is a cross of the previously described Campsis radicans and the Campsis grandiflora; the latter is not resistant to our winters, but the hybrid is. Like Campsis radicans, this one needs some support in the form of pins or wire. The plant must have good soil and a spot in the full sun. In this country it will only bloom fully in a hot summer, when it will create a lovely carpet of flowers.

CARYOPTERIS clandonensis 'Kew Blue'
Blue Spiraea

Flowering period: August to September.
Colour: dark blue(flower).
Height: 60 cm.
All types of soil are suitable for the caryopteris, but it must have a lot of sun. Its shape is circular and it has smooth-edged leaves. Its many dark blue flowers form on long, thin stems at a time when most shrubs have long since flowered. In the winter it dies right off, but reappears in early spring. It is a good idea therefore to cut it back to slightly above the ground.

CHAENOMELES japonica
Dwarf Quince

Flowering period: April.
Colour: orange-red(flower).
Height: 100 cm.
This dwarf bush, that comes from Japan, is usually grown from seed. It grows low and broad, is rather thorny, and has shiny, dark green, slightly serrated oval leaves. The strongly scented fruit is yellow-green with a red blush, and measures 4 cm across. It will grow in every garden soil but prefers to stand in the full sun.
To ensure a mass of flowers in the spring, it should be pruned during the summer.

CLEMATIS jackmannii
Clematis

Flowering period: June to August.
Colour: mauve.
Height: 2-3 metres(climber).
The clematis is a climber with strikingly large, deeply coloured flowers. The Clematis vitalba, the one closest to the wild variety, comes from the Caucasus. The jackmannii shown here is less sturdy than the Clematis vitalba but has much larger flowers. It grows well in chalky, slightly moist soil. To protect the roots from the full sun put creepers or stones round the foot of the plant. Prune in March or after flowering.

CLEMATIS 'Mme le Coultre'
Clematis

Flowering period: June to August.
Colour: white.
Height: 2-3 metres(climber).
This clematis has huge flowers, 8-10 cm across. It should be supported against a wall or fenze with twine or trellis work, preferably not facing due north or south. The foot of the plant should be protected from the sun. It needs moist, very chalky soil with loam. Make sure it is planted just in front of a wall, and not on the foundations. In March, or after flowering, prune away half the length of the plant.

CORNUS alba 'Elegantissima'
Dogwood

Flowering period: insignificant.
Colour: green with silvery edge(leaf).
Height: 250 cm.
This is the cultivated variety of the white Cornus that comes from Eastern Europe and North Asia. Its attraction comes not from its flowers, but from the furry summer leaf and the purple-red branches in winter. It will grow in either moist or dry soil, but preferably in the sun. To make the most of the winter colour of the bark plant several together in large groups. Prune well at the end of March.

CORNUS alba 'Sibirica'
Dogwood

Flowering period: insignificant.
Colour: green(leaf).
Height: 2 metres.
A cultivated white Cornus with a much tidier growth than others of its kind. It has oval leaves and, its most attractive feature, the winter bark of the young wood is coral. To make the most of this colour it is a good idea to plant a whole group together in an open space.
It prefers moist soil, although it will withstand dryness, and a sunny spot. It can be pruned in late March before the leaf forms.

CORYLUS maxima 'Purpurea'
Hazel

Flowering period: March.
Colour: russet(leaf), yellow-red(catkin).
Height: up to 2 metres.
Actually the Hazel should come under the heading 'Fruit trees' , but it is grown more for decoration than for its fruit. Plant it alone or in a group of shrubs. It likes any well drained soil and does very well in shade. Should you wish to grow it for its fruit, plant it near another Hazel: the resultant cross-pollination gives a higher yield of nuts.

COTINUS coggygria 'Royal Purple'
Smoke Bush

Flowering period: June to July.
Colour: dark red(flower).
Height: 2.5 metres.
This cultivated variety of the Cotinus will grow in any wet soil, in sun or partial shade. It is a fast grower more popular than others of its type because of its lovely, wine red leaf, which fades to a lighter red in the autumn. It has small flowers which bloom on 20 cm long, hairy stems. Plant it so that the colour of the leaf makes a nice contrast with other garden plants.

CLEMATIS
Clematis

The Clematis is a genuine woodland plant. Its scientific name comes from the Greek word 'klema' which means the tendril of a vine. Which brings us to the second important characteristic of the Clematis; it is a climber. Although this is not the case for every variety – and there are some 200 different types found throughout the whole world – it is true for the majority of Clematis, and it is the climbers that we describe here.

When growing wild, this plant flings itself upwards in search of the sun by winding its tendrils around trees and shurbs. In the garden, too, the Clematis must be planted in the shade and its tendrils trained towards the sun. This is because the foot of the plant must always be in shadow. It is a lovely plant to grow around the gable of your house, rich in beautiful flowers. Talk to your nurseryman so that you get a couple of early and a couple of late blooming plants, and you will have a Clematis that flowers for half the year. If you dot not want to create a flowery hedge, something for which the Clematis is also very suitable, and would rather just have it grow up against a wall, then it will need a bit of help. Unlike the ivy, it does not have very strong roots, but a few hooks and some vertically hung wire is enough. Unfortunately in winter it is an ugly, bare plant so it is a good idea to grow something colourful and leafy next to it. It is important to dig a wide and deep hole for the Clematis and to fill this with a mixture of old manure, peat mould, leaf mould and ordinary earth. Those that bloom early can be pruned after they have flowered; late bloomers in the spring.

A few of the varieties:
Clematis vitalba. This one also grows wild in some parts of the country. It reaches 15 metres in heigt and bloom from July to October with creamy white flowers, followed by silvery seedheads. In France it is known as 'herbe aux geux', beggars plant. This is because the sap from this Clematis causes festering wounds, and in earlier times the beggars of Paris tried to increase their pitiful appearance by using it. It is really only suitable for a natural garden, and must not be pruned.
Clematis alpina is the earliest blooming Clematis and reaches just two metres in height. It grows wild in Switzerland and blooms in April-May with bell-shaped, violet flowers. It is extremely winter resistant and can be left to climb over low walls or hedges.
Clematis orientalis grows to 4 metres and blooms with bell-shaped, yellow, individual flowers in August and September, followed by silvery seedheads. It has dense foliage of bluish-green, feathery leaves.
From the Himalayas comes the Clematis montana, a quick growing climber that can reach 9 metres in height. Its leaf is a shiny dark green with three segments, and it has masses of wide open, white flowers. Like its hybrids, it should not be pruned.
Clematis viticella has sprays of leaves, grows to 5 metres and blooms in late summer with mauve flowers that measure 4 cm.
Some of the large-flowered hybrid Clematis, usually not taller than 3 metres, are: Clematis 'Jackmanii', dark blue or purple, flowers from July to September.
Clematis 'Lasurstern', pale or dark blue, flowers from July to September.
'Ernest Markham', petunia red, flowers from July to September. 'Nelly Moser', lilac pink with a darker stripe, flowers from late May to July. 'Ville de Lyon', crimson, flowers from July to September. 'Lady Betty Balfour', violet with yellow stamen, flowers in September and October.

COTONEASTER conspicuus 'Decorus'
Cotoneaster

Flowering period: June.
Colour: white(blossom), orange-red(berry).
Height: up to 1 metre.
There are a great many varieties of Cotoneasters, and although this one is a dwarf, others grow to 4 metres in height. In addition, some are evergreen, some partly evergreen and some deciduous.
The 'Decorus' belongs to the evergreen variety; the leaves are small and form a dense growth along the branches which curve outwards under the weight of the hundreds of orange-red berries. The Cotoneaster makes no special demands on the soil or the surroundings.

COTONEASTER horizontalis
Cotoneaster

Flowering period: June.
Colour: white to soft pink(blossom), deep red(berry), green(summer leaf), red(autumn leaf).
Height: 50-75 cm tall, by up to 3 metres wide.
The Cot. horizontalis belongs to the deciduous group, but the bush is never completely bare as it is covered in red berries from September until the spring. Because the small branches fan outwards, it is often used to cover a wall. It can also be used as a creeper in flowerbeds or rock gardens. It makes few demands although it will not withstand severe frost.

COTONEASTER watereri 'Cornubia'
Cotoneaster

Flowering period: June.
Colour: white(blossom), red(berry).
Height: 2-4 metres tall, by up to 4 metres wide.
This is the tallest of all the partly evergreen Cotoneasters. After it has flowered in June, the berries form in bunches that hang from the branches. At the same time, the leaves reach their full size (up to 10 cm in length). Berries and leaves remain on the bush through the winter.
The berries are very popular with the birds. Like the other Cotoneasters, it makes no special demands on soil or surroundings, but it does like the full sun.

CYTISUS praecox
Broom

Flowering period: April to May.
Colour: creamy white.
Height: 1 to 2 metres.
It is broom, with its mass of flowers, that signals the arrival of summer. It is a peculiar shrub that actually consists of a collection of individual branches on which the flowers appear.
After it has bloomed, it is just and ordinary green bush for the rest of the year. It prefers to grow in sandy soil, but also does well in light, well drained earth in full sun. It looks particularly nice in rock and heather gardens.

CYTISUS preacox 'Allgold'
Broom

Flowering period: April to May.
Colour: yellow.
Height: 1 to 2 metres.
The difference between this broom and the previous one is its size and the colour of its flowers. The flower of Cyt. 'Allgold' is slightly larger and the colour is deep yellow.
Broom is easy to propagate from the seed which can be taken from the seedpods once these are ripe. It is an attractive plant not only because of the deep colour of its flowers but also because of their fragrance. But its appearance belies the fact that it is poisonous.

CYTISUS preacox 'Hollandia'
Broom

Flowering period: early May.
Colour: mauve.
Height: 1 to 3 metres.
To obtain a frost resistant red broom the (frost resistant) Cyt. praecox is crossed with the (less hardy) Cyt. burkwoodii: the best of the resulting hybrids is the 'Hollandia', a broom with mauve flowers. To make sure that this rather tall shrub does not become straggly, it should be cut back after flowering. Like the other types of broom, this one grows in just about any well drained soil, but it does prefer sandy ground.

DAPHNE mezereum
Pepper Tree

Flowering period: March to April.
Colour: pale and deep mauve(flower).
Height: 100 cm.
Despite its name, the pepper tree has nothing to do with the pepper that comes from the tropics.
The bright red berries of this bush are extremely poisonous and this makes it a danger for small children. Indigenous to Europe and Central Asia, it has thin, 3-8 cm long, grey-green leaves which it sheds in autumn. It prefers chalky soil with humus which should be moist but not wet, and a spot in the full sun.

DEUTZIA gracilis
Deutzia

Flowering period: May to June.
Colour: white(flower).
Height: 75 cm.
The deutzia takes its name from the Dutchman Johan Deutz. This one comes from Japan and has 5-7 cm long leaves that are dark green, thin and serrated. In the winter it is an unremarkable, leafless, woody brown bush. It blooms in small upright sprays of tiny round flowers. It grows in any ground but prefers fertile soil in the sun or partial shade. To keep it nice it should be pruned every other year.

ERICA carnea
Heath

Flowering period: January to April.
Colour: white, pink, red.
Height: 20 cm.
This one comes from the Alps where in winter it transforms whole areas into carpets of flowers. Its stiff, needle-like leaves grow in garlands around the branches, and do not fall in winter.
They make a lovely contrast with the small, bell shaped flowers. It blooms more fully in the sun and, unlike most heather, will grow in slightly chalky soil. You will find a huge selection of this cultivated heather in garden centres and nurseries.

EUONYMUS europeus
Cardinals Hat

Flowering period: May.
Colour: yellow-green(flower), pink(fruit).
Height: 4-5 metres.
This tall shrub or small tree has very pretty fruit and leaves but rather unremarkable flowers.
The leaves are oval, slightly serrated and bright green in colour, turning to pink in the autumn before they fall. The fruit, which does indeed look like a cardinal's hat, has orange seeds and is poisonous. It can be planted in the shade, preferably several together for cross-pollination.

EUONYMUS planipes
Cardinals Hat

Flowering period: May.
Colour: yellow-green(flower), deep red(fruit).
Height: 4-5 metres.
This Euonymus comes from Japan. It, too, is a sturdy, broad and bushy shrub that can be planted in groups or on its own. The 8-12 cm long, oval leaf is slightly serrated and a fresh green colour. In autumn it turns a lovely red. Although the individual flowers are unexciting, the shrub in full bloom is a feast for the eyes. The red, poisonous fruit appears in September-October. It can be propagated from seeds and cuttings.

FORSYTHIA
Forsythia

Flowering period: April.
Colour: yellow(flower).
Height: 2.5 to 3 metres.
Very few English gardens do not have a forsythia. Its striking, vivid yellow flower must persuade even the biggest pessimist that spring has arrived. Its large number of bell shaped flowers form in the two or more year old wood. During the summer it is just an ordinary dark green leafy plant. There are many different varieties in the shops, all of which need well drained, fertile and chalky soil.

GENISTA tinctoria
Broom

Flowering period: June to August.
Colour: golden yellow(flower).
Height: 1 metre.
This is a very upright shrub with green branches, indigenous to Europe and Asia Minor. Its 1-2.5 cm long leaves are thin and elliptical with a fresh green colour. The flowers hang from the ends of the branches in sprays of 6 cm or more in length.
It needs a light, loose and warm soil in the full sun, and should be well pruned ever so often.
Keep an eye on small children as the plant is poisonous.

GINKGO biloba
Ginkgo

Flowering period: insignificant.
Colour: bright green(leaf).
Height: 4-6 metres in 10-15 years.
This tree dates from prehistoric times and is only found growing wild in China. The oldest in Europe is probably the one in the botanical gardens in Utrecht in the Netherlands, which was planted in 1735. It can grow to 30 metres tall and its branches, which are thick and stiff, are few in number. The shape varies from thin and vertical to broad with a round crown. The leathery, fan-shaped leaves turn golden yellow in the autumn.

HAMAMELIS intermedia 'Feuerzauber'
Hamamelis

Flowering period: January to March.
Colour: deep orange-red(flower).
Height: 2-3 metres.
This is a hybrid from the Japanese and the Chinese Hamamelis, and is one of the earliest blooming garden shrubs. Its bright green leaf is oval and veined. It does not grow very fast but patience is rewarded by its nice shape and lovely flowers.
It looks very pretty when grown as a contrast to the Chinese Hamamelis with its canary yellow flowers. It grows in ordinary, well drained soil, and does not need pruning.

HEDERA helix 'Hibernica'
Irish Ivy

Flowering period: insignificant.
Colour: dark green with white veins(leaf).
Height: 20 metres.
It will only reach this height if it is grown against a wall. If there is no obstacle in the way, it will just spread itself across the earth, which makes it a very good creeper. The segmented, 10-15 cm long leaf is bigger than that of the ordinary ivy but with smaller segments. It loves shade. Used as a covering for an old fence, it provides the garden with a lovely patch of greenery all through the year.

HIBISCUS syriacus 'Red Heart'
Hibiscus

Flowering period: August to October.
Colour: white with a red centre(flower).
Height: 1.5 to 2 metres.
There are about 200 varieties of the hibiscus, which is found growing wild only in China and North India. This one is a round, upright shrub with grey branches. The leaf, with its three segments, is a fresh green colour, 4-8 cm long, and looks rather like an oak leaf. It blooms very late, so if the weather turns cold the flowers will not come fully out. For this reason, plant it in the sunniest and most sheltered part of the garden.

HIBISCUS syriacus 'Woodbridge'
Hibiscus

Flowering period: August to October.
Colour: deep red with a dark centre(flower).
Height: 2 metres.
Like the previous cultivated hibiscus this one, too, needs a sunny, sheltered spot in order to bloom fully in the late summer. Young plants must be protected in harsh winters. The older and more woody it is, the better it withstands winter weather. As it blooms on the one year old wood, it can be cut well back in early spring.
It prefers fresh, loose, fertile and well drained soil.

HYDRANGEA macrophylla
Hydrangea

Flowering period: August to September.
Colour: white, pink, red, blue(flower).
Height: 1 to 1.8 metres.
Although the Hydrangea macrophylla is actually the houseplant of this family, it can also be grown in the garden, but it is not entirely winter resistant. The advantage of hydrangeas is that they bloom late and for a long time and, unlike most shrubs, they flower in the shade.
After flowering, it must be cut back to just above the old wood. It does best in moist, chalky soil.

HYDRANGEA paniculata 'Grandiflora'
Hydrangea

Flowering period: August.
Colour: (green-) white, turning to pink.
Height: 2-3 metres, by the same width.
If the previous Hydrangea, the marcophylla, is really more of a houseplant, the Hydrangea paniculata is the genuine garden variety. For many years it was only found in farmyards but it is more common these days often seen growing alone or in groups.
It needs a moist, humus rich soil in a shady spot. Once fully out the flowers can be dried. Cut the bush back to the old wood in the spring.

HYPERICUM calycinum
St. John's Wort

Flowering period: July to August.
Colour: golden yellow(flower).
Height: 20-30 cm.
The Germans believed that hypericum would protect their houses from being struck by lightning, and in Silesia it was thought to be an oracle: a magical plant. This one comes from South-East Europe and Asia Minor. It has a very bushy growth and oval, leathery, dark green leaves which it keeps in winter. Because it quickly forms a thick, mat-like covering, it is a fine creeper, especially in partial shade. It grows in all soils.

ILEX aquifolium
Holly

Flowering period: May to June.
Colour: shiny dark green(leaf), red(fruit).
Height: 10-15 metres.
There are about 400 different types of holly which are found in just about all parts of the world. This is the ordinary, prickly holly that grows wild in Britain. It is a slow grower and its evergreen leaves are extremely sharp. Its flowers are a dirty white, and it is the leaves and the lovely red berries, that remain on the bush well into the winter, that make it so attractive. It grows in all soils, preferably in full or partial shade.

KERRIA japonica 'Pleniflora'
Jew's Mallow

Flowering period: May to July.
Colour: saffron yellow(flower).
Height: 2 metres.
This is the double-flowered Kerria that, unlike the similar but single-flowered variety, does not grow in the wild. It is a shrub that grows straight upwards with green, pithy branches and oval, pointed and serrated leaves with slightly hairy undersides. The dead flowers must be cut off, and every three years the whole shrub should be pruned down to the ground. It prefers a warm spot in good soil.

KOLKWITZIA amabilis
Beauty Bush

Flowering period: late May to June.
Colour: pink(flower).
Height: 2.5 to 3 metres.
There is just one variety of this lovely shrub.
It comes from West China where it grows to a height of 3,000 metres, which is why it easily withstands the harshest winter. Because it grows as broad as it does tall, it needs a lot of space.
It is an attractive bush with overhanging branches and dull green, oval leaves that grow in pairs. Its luxuriant bloom forms clouds of tiny pink flowers.

HYDRANGEA
Hydrangea

Hydrangeas grow wild in parts of America and Asia. Most of them bloom in late summer when the majority of shrubs have already formed their fruit. They also differ from most other flowering trees and bushes in preferring to stand in full or partial shade, although some varieties can withstand the full sun as long as they are kept well watered. The many large blooms of the Hydrangea are actually two flowers in one. The centre is a small, uninteresting but fertile flower. Around this is a large, striking but sterile flower, that probably just has the job of attracting insects. And people, too, of course: for some years the Hydrangea lost some of its popularity and was only found growing in farmyards, but it is now regaining its appeal. In general, the leaves are large, oval and soft to the touch, and vary in colour from pale to dark green. All Hydrangeas need fertile, moist and chalk free soil. If the plant does not grow properly and the leaf begins to turn yellow, then it needs some extra plant food. Feed it whith a bit of iron sulphate dissolved in water, or with some bone meal. Both of these will also deepen the colour of plants that have blue flowers. Hydrangeas that are left unpruned will bloom with just one or two large and lots of smaller flowers. It is therefore better to cut away the buds at the ends of strong shoots so that those underneath fill out properly, thus creating a much more balanced bloom. Dead wood should also be cut away in order to give the plant more space and light.

Hydrangea macrophylla, the well known indoor variety, becomes a garden plant simply by being planted outdoors, although it is not strictly necessary, because there are more than enough true garden Hydrangeas.

Hydragea arborescens 'Grandiflora' blooms with wide, white and sterile double flowers, from July to September. Hydrangea paniculata 'Grandiflora', also white, but easy to recognise because of its pear-shaped, also sterile, sprays of flowers. These are so heavy that the branches bend under their weight. Much prettier than the sterile Hydrangeas, however, are the ones that have two types of flower in one. Like the Hydrangea serrata 'Acuminata', with steel blue, fertile little flowers in the centre, surrounded by deep pink petals. It is a really beautiful Hydrangea but it grows very slowly and no higher than 1.5 metres. The Hydrangea sargentiana that comes from China grows to a height of 2 metres and has large, velvety, emerald green leaves. Its double flower consists of lots of little lilac flowers surrounded by large white or pink sterile petals.

It appears to die off completely in winter, but there is no need to worry because it will regrow. There is just one climbing Hydrangea: the Hydragea petiolaris from Japan where it can be found growing to the top of the trees by means of its tendrils. In gardens in this country it will certainly reach a height of 10 metres. The flowers are completely white, consisting of small fertile flowers and single, long, pointed and sterile petals. This one will even grow over a north facing wall, and if you let it curl its way up the trees in the garden, it will do them no harm.

LABURNUM watereri 'Vossii'
Laburnum or Golden Rain

Flowering period: April to May.
Colour: yellow.
Height: 5-8 metres.
This shrub-like tree is a cross between the ordinary golden rain and the alpine golden rain.
It grows very quickly and is the most beautiful of the laburnums, hence its great popularity. It looks lovely when contrasted with blue and violet syringa which flowers during the same period. It does well in any soil containing some chalk but prefers a sunny spot. Because it is a hybrid it cannot be propagated from seed. Golden rain is poisonous.

LIGUSTRUM ovalifolium
Privet

Flowering period: July.
Colour: white(flower), black(berry), green(leaf).
Height: up to 5 metres.
Many people are unaware that this shrub has flowers because it is generally trimmed before it can bloom. Privet is predominantly used as a hedge; trimmed three times a year to form a neat barrier that ensures privacy. It makes absolutely no demands and remains partly green, although it is not completely winter resistant; in fact, if the frost attacks it, it is better to cut it right back to its base.

LONICERA periclymenum
Wood Honeysuckle

Flowering period: June to August.
Colour: yellow-white(flower).
Height: 3 metres.
There are 180 different known varieties of the honeysuckle, of which about half grow in the wild. They can be divided into three groups: climbers; small leafed evergreens; and deciduous honey suckle. Here we are concerned only with the climbers. This one has the strongest scent of all honeysuckles, particularly in the early morning and at sunset, and as long as it grows in moist soil.

LONICERA periclymenum 'Belgica'
Wood Honeysuckle

Flowering period: May to June.
Colour: mauve; yellow inside(flower).
Height: 3 metres.
This is a cultivated variety of the wood honeysuckle. It grows a little slower than the others and also had slightly ticker leaves. It blooms earlier but just as richly as all honeysuckles.
The flowers are tubular or trumpet shaped and form in sprays. Never allow a honeysuckle to wind itself around a young tree because the tendrils have no give in them and will strangle it.

LONICERA tellmanniana
Honeysuckle

Flowering period: May to July.
Colour: yellow-orange(flower)
Height: 5-6 metres.
This one is a climber, as sweet smelling and rich in flower as the previous two. The leaves, which grow in pairs, are 5-10 cm long ovals, deep green on the top with a frosty white underside. The tubular flowers grow in thick sprays at the end of the branches. Once the flowers are over, large coral berries appear. The plant is poisonous. Honeysuckle grows in all moist soils, and is easy to propagate from cuttings.

MAGNOLIA liliflora 'Nigra'
Magnolia

Flowering period: late May.
Colour: dark purple(flower)
Height: 3 metres.
This is a broad shrub with few branches and has the darkest flowers of all the magnolias. These measure 12 cm in length, grow vertically and are a thin bell shape. Usually it flowers for a second time later in the season, but with fewer blooms. The 10-15 cm long, oval leaf is a shiny dark green and appears at the same time as the flower. It shows to best advantage when it stands alone and in the full sun.

MAGNOLIA soulangiana
Magnolia

Flowering period: May.
Colour: pinky white.
Height: 6 metres.
This magnolia blooms even before the leaves appear with large, vertical, bell-like flowers.
It is a woody shrub with a broad growth and therefore needs a lot of space; to which it does full justice. The oval or elliptical leaf is completely green, although the top is darker than the underneath. The magnolia must have fertile, slightly acid soil with humus, a lot of sun and plenty of water during hot spells.

MAHONIA aquifolium 'Apollo'
Oregon Grape

Flowering period: April to May.
Colour: yellow(flower), dark purple(berry), dark green(leaf), red(winter leaf).
Height: up to 1 metre.
A native of North America, the Mahonia is a low growing, evergreen shrub that makes virtually no demands on soil or surroundings. Because of this it is very suitable for flowerbeds and parks, either as a background for other plants or to create a flowery wall. It will also flourish in both shade and full sun. Its yellow flowers and purple berries make it very attractive.

MAHONIA bealei
Mahogany

Flowering period: April.
Colour: yellow(flower).
Height: 2 metres.
There was a time when mahogany trees were often planted in the parks in this country, but they seem to have lost some of their popularity. This may be because they grow rather slowly. Green in winter, it has oval, moss green leaves with a couple of sharp thorns on either side. The blooms with vertical sprays of tiny flowers, followed by blue berries that can be used for jam making or fruit drinks.

MALUS moerlandsii 'Profusion'
Ornamental Apple

Flowering period: mid-May to early June.
Colour: purple-red(blossom), dark red(fruit).
Height: 3-4 metres.
A large garden is the best place for this ornamental apple, that cannot really be called either a tree or a shrub: too big for one, too small for the other. Its sturdy branches and mass of blossom make it a feast for the eyes when it flowers in spring. For the best result, plant it alone in fertile, well drained soil in the full sun. If the soil is sandy, it will occasionally need to be fertilised.

PASSIFLORA caerulea
Passion Flower

Flowering period: summer and autumn.
Colour: greenish white with blue and purple.
Height: about 3 metres.
The legendary passion flower is a tropical climbing shrub that grows wild in the eastern part of South American right up into Central America. In this country it can be grown in the garden from May to Ocotber, but it needs a sunny, sheltered spot. For the rest of the year keep it indoors or in a greenhouse. The large, individual flowers are breathtakingly beautiful. In summer give it plenty of water and fertiliser, but in winter very little. It can be pruned in spring.

PERNETTYA mucronata
Prickly Heath

Flowering period: May to June.
Colour: white(flower), white, pink, red(fruit).
Height: 0.5 to 1 metres.
This is a small evergreen shrub indigenous to South America, particularly Tierra del Fuego. The pitcher-shaped flowers are extremely tiny, but so many in number that during the flowering period the plant looks lovely. However, the main attraction is its coloured berries that remain for most of the winter. It needs a lightly shaded spot – for instance, underneath rhododendrons – and cool, moist soil mixed with leaf mould or peat.

PHILADELPHUS lemoinei
Jasmine

Flowering period: June to July.
Colour: white(flower).
Height: 1.8 metres.
This is the well known strongly perfumed jasmine that adds a touch of romance to moonlit nights. This one is excellent for the garden and is named after the French nurseryman Lemoine. It is a very pretty shrub, with upright branches that later droop, and bright green, ribbed and oval leaves. It is a feast for the eyes when in bloom, but in winter it is just a mass of bare, dead branches. It grows in all soils.

PIERIS japonica 'Forest Flame'
Andromeda

Flowering period: April to May.
Colour: white(flower).
Height: 3 metres.
Like all these Japanese Pieris, this one also blooms in downward hanging sprays of tiny, cup-shaped flowers at the end of the one year old branches. It is a sturdy shrub and is extremely winter resistant. The young shoots are red and, depending on age, the leaf has a whole series of colours: red, pink, cream and green. It does not shed its leaves in winter, and prefers shade and acid, peaty soil.

PIERIS japonica 'Variegata'
Andromeda

Flowering period: March to May.
Colour: white(flower).
Height: 1.5 to 3 metres.
This is an evergreen, dwarf variety of the Pieris that comes from Japan. The tiny, cup-shaped flowers grow in downward hanging sprays. Its very thin, leathery leaf has a white edge and when fully out is slightly pink though basically a shiny green. Because it is a plant that likes light shade and moist, acid, humus rich soil, it is a good idea to combine it with the rhododendron. It is easy to propagate from cuttings.

POLYGONUM aubertii
Knotgrass

Flowering period: June to October.
Colour: greenish white(flower).
Height: 15 metres (climber).
If you have a bare wall to your house which you would like to cover quickly, or an ugly shed that could do with some decoration, there is no better choice than knotgrass. It comes from West China and Tibet and is the fastest growing, most winter resistant climber there is. The bright green leaf is heart shaped, and the flowers form in long sprays at the ends of the branches. Keep an eye on it, though, so that it does not strangle any of the trees in your garden.

PRUNUS
Prunus

There are some two hundred different varieties of flowering cherry all of which are indigenous to the temperate zones of the northern hemisphere. They are trees or shrubs that differ rather a lot, but they do have one thing in common: they all bear fruit with stones. Although 'stones' is not perhaps the right word, since the fruit of the Prunus is fleshy and juicy and the stone is just a very hard pip that is, in fact, the seed. However, there is no need to go into details about the fruit because everyone knows cherries, plums and peaches. The flowers, generally white or pink but occasionally yellow, have five sepals and five petals, one pistil and many stamen. They differ in this from appel or pear blossoms which have five pistils in each flower. To make things easier, the Prunus family can be divided into two large groups: the first includes all those grown especially for their fruit; the second covers the ornamental trees and shrubs. Here we shall only describe a number of the latter. They are all easy to grow, winter resistant trees or shrubs that make no special demands on the soil, except that this must contain a small amount of chalk. In addition, they generally prefer to stand in the sun.

Prunus avium, the sweet cherry, is the predecessor of many well known types of cherry.

Indigenous to Europe, it has oval, coarsely serrated leaves that turn red or yellow in autumn. As the leaf appears, it also blooms with open, white flowers. The edible cherries are very dark red. Even more beautiful is the cultivated Prunus avium 'Plena' with its mass of blossom. It is a very tall (15 metres) but also extremely sturdy flowering cherry. The Prunus cerasifera is the plum, of which the 'Nigra' is particularly recommended. This grows to a heigt of 5-7 metres with a round crown, and has dark red leaves and pale pink, short and pointed flowers. The flowering cherries popular with the birds grow well in full or partial shade. Of these, the ordinary Prunus padus and the American Prunus serotina are grown in this country. They bloom in sparys of tiny white flowers. This type of flowering cherry is often planted in woods because it improves the soil for other trees. However, the disadvantage is that it quickly dominates its surroundings.

Prunus laurocerasus and Prunus lusitanica, the ordinary laurel cherry and the Portugese laurel cherry, are grown for their leaf. Both are evergreens with huge, shiny, leathery leaves. The Portugese laurel cherry is slightly less hardy and does not withstand winter weather so well. Very pretty is the Prunus laurocerasus 'Otto Luyken', a thick, broad bush that grows to one metre in heigt, and blooms in rich sprays of tiny white flowers. Prunus serrulata, the Japanese flowering cherry, is without doubt the most important of the ornamental cherries. There is a large number of cultivated varieties, one of which is found in just about every garden: the Prunus serrulata 'Kanzan'. It is a tree that grows up to a height of 12 metres with a funnel shaped crown. In early May it puts forth an unbelievably rich blossom of double pink flowers.

Its green leaf turns russet in autumn.

Prunus persica is probably the forerunner of the cultivated peach. The most popular ornamental peach seems to be the Prunus persica 'Klara Meyer' with its bright pink double flowers. Its fruit, too, is good to eat. The little almond tree, Prunus triloba, that grows to just two metres, has some of spring's most beautiful blossom. Its double flowers are bright pink.

The Prunus subhirtella 'Autumnalis' is a five metres tall tree with outspread branches, and a most remarkable flowering pattern. It blooms in October-November with white or pale pink flowers, and then again in April but this time with pure pink blossom.

POTENTILLA fruticosa
Shrubby Cinquefoil

Flowering period: June to October.
Colour: (gold-)yellow.
Height: 80-120 cm, and about the same in width.
Because this plant was originally uncultivated and comes from the far northern hemisphere, it does well in this country. It makes no demands except for a sunny spot. These useful qualities and its dense growth make it popular for public parks and also for hedges. To prevent it from running wild, it is recommended that the bush is well pruned in March. The shrubby cinquefoil sheds its leaves in winter.

POTENTILLA fruticosa 'Abbotswood'
Shrubby Cinquefoil

Flowering period: June to October.
Colour: white.
Height: 80-120 cm.
Just like the previous shrubby cinquefoil, the 'Abbotswood' is a particularly sturdy and easy to grow shrub, that grows in just about any soil and withstands dryness. It should be pruned in March to keep its shape. There is a large selection of cinque-foils available which vary in colour and height. The height varies from 30 cm to 1.2 metres, while the colour can be yellow, white or pale orange. It is very suitable for hedges or borders.

PRUNUS cistena
Flowering Cherry

Flowering period: April to May.
Colour: pale pink(blossom), dark red(leaf).
Height: 1-2 metres.
The family of Prunus contains hundreds of trees and shrubs that vary considerably in shape and flower: from drooping to ball shaped; from white to red blossoms; from dwarf bush to tree; from fruit tree to ornamental shrub; all occur in this family. Like most Prunus, this one needs chalky, well drained soil and full sun. It is sturdy, and its dense growth and beautiful blossom turn a hedge into a wall of colour.

PRUNUS serrulata 'Kiku-shidare-sakura'
Japanese Flowering Cherry

Flowering period: April.
Colour: pink(blossom), (bronze)-green(leaf).
Height: 1.5 to 4 metres.
Of de Japanese flowering cherries this 'Kiku-shidare-sakura' is one of the most popular because of its lovely drooping shape and large flowers. Like most of the Prunus family, it makes few demands: a sunny spot in chalky, well drained soil is enough. Because of its lovely shape it looks best when standing alone, on a lawn or a patio. All Japanese flowering cherries are frost resistant and withstand a city atmosphere.

PYRACANTHA 'Orange Glow'
Pyracanthus

Flowering period: May to June.
Colour: white(blossom), orange(berry).
Height: 2-3 metres(espalier).
From mid-September to December the Pyracantha looks lovely with its mass of brightly coloured berries. Because it stays green the whole year it makes a nice covering for a wall, and with some support will grow up to 3 metres tall. It needs good soil; it is a good idea to dig a fair size hole next to the plant and fill this with leaf mould. It also needs to stand in the full sun. It is easy to propagate from cuttings.

RHODODENDRON-hybrid
Rhododendron

Flowering period: April to May.
Colour: pink, yellow, mauve, red, blue, white.
Height: 80 cm to 3 metres.
Rhododendrons offer a huge choice of hybrids with flowers in all shapes and colours. They are very popular for dividing up parks and large gardens. To ensure the fullest flowering, plant them in moist, well drained, chalk free soil; they will not withstand full sun. Early bloomers must be protected from the north and east winds, and also from frost. Rhododendrons are lovely planted in groups with different flowering times.

RHODODENDRON-hybrid 'Linda'
Rhododendron

Flowering period: mid-May.
Colour: pinky red.
Height: 50 cm to 1 metre.
'Linda' is a fairly new hybrid obtained from the Rhododendron williansianum. This latter is quite a low growing shrub with very few flowers and rather sensitive to frost. Many growers have tried to improve on these points resulting in countless hybrids, of which 'Linda' is one. The same instructions apply as for the previous rhododendron, but we should add that it flowers more fully when the dead blooms are cut off.

RHODODENDRON-hybrid 'Scarlet Wonder'
Rhododendron

Flowering period: May to June.
Colour: scarlet.
Height: 50-80 cm.
'Scarlet Wonder' is another low growing rhododendron. The flowers are evenly spread over the whole bush, which is quite different from other rhododendrons where they grow in groups. This one is better for combining with other shrubs than the taller varieties. A number of rhododendrons retain some of their leaves; those leaves that do fall should be left around the bush as food and protection from frost.

RHODODENDRON
Rhododendron

This is a very extensive family of plants with about a thousand known varieties. Many are evergreen, but there are also quite a few that shed their leaf in winter; for example, most of the Azaleas which also belong to the Rhododendron family but are described in a seperate section. Some come from the north-east part of North America, a few from the Caucasus, just two are indigenous to Europe, and the rest come from Asia. In particular, many varieties of wild Rhododendron, and even some natural hybrids, grow in the Himalayas, in the high reaches of Tibet, and in the West China provinces of Yunnan and Szettsjwan. At the end of the previous century British and American botanists organised special expeditions to these areas to look for Rhododendrons. We have these people to thank for the many lovely winter resistant varieties and hybrids that really should be grown in every garden. The leaves of the Rhododendron are generally oval, leathery and grow singly. They often form garlands around the ends of the boughs. The flowers are tubular, funnel or bell shaped, usually forming in fairly tight sprays. When the uninteresting fruit is ripe, it bursts and scatters its fine, winged seed into the air.
Rhododendrons grow best in full or partial shade, although a few garden hybrids can withstand the full

sun as long as the soil is kept moist. What they must have, however, is well drained, fertile, acid and chalk free soil. So if your garden is made up of heavy clay, do not even consider growing Rhododendrons. Pruning can be limited to the straggly branches. But do cut off the dead flowers, otherwise the plant will lose a lot of energy in forming seed and will not bloom so fully. And if there are too many buds on the plant in early spring, a number of these can be cut away so that those that do bloom form a much bigger flower.
Some of the large-flowered, tall (2-4 metres) garden hybrids are: with white flowers – Rhododendron 'Bismarck', 'Catawbiense Album', 'Cunningham's White', 'Gomer Waterer', 'Jacksonii', 'Caucasicum', 'Belle Heller'. With pink flowers – 'Scintillation', 'Le Progres', 'Hugo de Vries', 'Parsons Gloriosum', 'Lady Annette de Trafford', 'Furnivall's Daughter'. With purple or pale mauve flowers – 'Alfred', 'Catawbiense Boursault', 'Catawbiense Grandiflora', 'Everestianum', 'Fastuosum Flore Pleno', 'Humboldt', 'Lee's Dark Purple', 'Purpureum Elegans', 'Williams Campanulatum Hybrid'. With red flowers – 'Van Weerden Poelman', 'Old Port', 'Nova Zembla', 'Mrs P. den Ouden', 'Edward S. Rand', 'Dr. H.C. Dresselhuys', 'Caractacus', 'Brittania'.
The 'Flava' and the 'Goldsworth Yellow' have yellow flowers, and 'Blue Peter' is lavender blue with a dark red fleck.
Of the Rhododendron williamsianum hybrids, that grow to 1 to 1.5 metres, we recommend 'Vater Böhlje' (lilac-pink), 'Görlitz' (bright pink), 'Lissabon' (pinky red), 'Jackwill' (pale pink). If you have a small garden, plant just one of the dwarf Rhododendrons that grow no higher than 1 metre: 'Baden-Baden', 'Scarlet Wonder', 'Elizabeth Hobbie', 'Bengal', 'Mannheim'. They all have lovely, red flowers.
Some of the pretty wild ones are: Rhododendron ferrugineum, the Alpine rose that also grows in the Pyrenese and the Apennines. It blooms in June with tiny purple-red flowers. Rhododendron minus, from America, 1.5 metres tall with lilac pink flowers. Rhododendron russatum from China, 1 metre tall with dark mauve flowers. Rhododendron wardi from China and south east Tibet, 2 metres tall with large, bright yellow flowers. Rhododendron smirnowii from the Caucasus, 2-3 metres tall with medium sized pink flowers.

RIBES sanguineum
Flowering Currant

Flowering period: April to May.
Colour: dark red(blossom), green(summer leaf), yellow/red(autumn leaf).
Height: 1-2 metres.
The flowering currant belongs to the same family as the gooseberry and the blackberry, but it is also used a lot in gardens and parks for its decorative appearance. The beautiful blossom looks particularly nice in combination with the forsythia, which blooms at the same time. The flowering currant grows in any good, well drained soil and is frost resistant. The sturdiest and most beautiful is Rib. sang. 'King Edward VII'.

ROSA floribunda
Floribunda Rose

Flowering period: July to October.
Colour: yellow, red, orange, pink.
Height: 80 cm to 1 metre.
With at least 200 varieties of rose from which to choose, it is impossible to give here a proper impression of the choice available. But we can show some of the main classifications: floribunda, tea and climber. We make this distinction for practical reasons; it is not official. You will find the dog or wild rose under fruit because of its hips. Below is some information on rose growing.

ROSA hybrid Tearose
Tearose

Flowering period: July to October.
Colour: very varied.
Height: 60 to 100 cm.
Unlike the floribunda rose, the hybrid tea does not have a very rich bloom but the flowers are large and almost perfect. Roses like fertile, airy, slightly lime rich soil. They do not like a too acid soil or a lot of moisture. They grow best in a moderately sheltered and sunny spot.
Depending on their eventual height, bush roses should be planted at 40-80 cm intervals. Full blown flowers and suckers should be cut off.

ROSA
Climber Rose

Flowering period: June to October.
Colour: white, pink, red, yellow.
Height: 2-3 metres(climber).
As well as the floribunda and hybrid tea, there is a third type of rose: the climber, another large group of varying types. It needs trellis or wire up which to climb, and can be grown against walls, sheds, fences, pergolas, etc. This one grows well in sun or shade, but it blooms better in the sun. Like the other roses, the climber appreciates an annual treatment of manure in November.

SALIX caprea 'Pendula'
Willow

Flowering period: March to April.
Colour: silver grey(catkin), dull green(leaf).
Height: 1 to 3 metres.
The height of this weeping willow depends on just where it is grafted onto the trunk. In principle, an old willow of this type can reach 6-8 metres, but most remain low and are therefore very suitable for the small garden. To prevent the branches from becoming lank, they should be well pruned each year (in April). Because of its special shape, it is better to plant it alone. It makes no special demands on soil or surroundings.

SALIX matsudana 'Tortuosa'
Willow

Flowering period: March to April.
Colour: silver grey(catkin), grey green(leaf).
Height: 1 to 1.5 metres in 10 years, up to 7 m.
In general this willow is kept small otherwise it loses its twisted shape after about five years. Grow a small tree from a cutting and you get the same corkscrew effect; prune it every year (in April) so that it keeps its beautiful shape. The willow grows best in clay or marshy soil – it is not *the* waterside tree for nothing. But it will also do well in other soils because it is a particularly sturdy tree. It is often seen along roads and rivers.

SAMBUCUS nigra
Elder

Flowering period: June to July.
Colour: white(flower), dark blue(fruit).
Height: up to 7 metres.
The elder grows wild from Europe to Siberia. Because it is a very sturdy tree, almost as persistent as a weed, it grows anywhere; but if you want it to bloom as fully as possible, plant it in fertile soil with lime. The flowers can be used for brewing tea, and the berries for making syrup, jam and wine. In fact, the berries are medicinal and help to prevent constipation, heart disease and influenza. Prune in spring.

SKIMMIA japonica 'Rubella'
Skimmia

Flowering period: May.
Colour: yellow-green(blossom), coral(berry).
Height: up to 1 metre.
The Skimmia japonica is a round, rather low bush. The most striking thing about it is the perfume of its flowers, rather than the colour of its leaf, berry or flower. It is an evergreen shrub that does well in our climate. In winter it has a light covering of berries, but it is mainly used as a background – it does well in the shade – or for the border. It does best in fertile, loamy soil or sandy ground rich in humus.

ROSA
Rose

There have been roses on Earth for thousands of years. In fact, fossilised remains more than thirty million years old have been found in America. And there are countless varieties.

Roses grow wild all over the northern hemisphere, but south of the equator there are just four different types. Without doubt, the rose is the most loved of all plants because of its wonderful scent and the special beauty of its flowers. Five hundred years before Christ, Herodotus was already describing roses in the garden of King Midas. Cleopatra received her lover Marcus Antonius in a room carpeted with rose petals. There is no other flower that speaks so directly to the imagination or is so laden with simbolism as the rose. When Mitterand won the French general election in 1982, people went out onto the streets with a red rose in their hands. Red roses are the gift of lovers. Back in the Middle Ages there were already royal houses which had the rose as their emblem. At the beginning of the nineteenth century the Empress Josephine of France had a collection of some two hundred varieties in her palace gardens. And the garden is still the basis for today's rose growers, although the days when roses were grown exclusively for kings and emperors are long gone. The different varieties can be classified as follows: 1. *Tea rose.* These bloom with full, large and individual flowers, although not in great profusion. 2. *Floribunda rose.* Here the single or double flowers form in sprays. They are less beautiful than the tea rose, but much more abundant. 3. *Climbing rose.* This has a profusion of single or double individual flowers but a short flowering period. 4. *Rambler.* Another climbing rose, but whith masses of tiny flowers in sprays. 5. *Miniature rose.* The dwarf version of the floribunda, no taller than 30 cm. 6. *Standard rose.* This is usually a hybrid tea rose that has been grafted onto the stem of a briar. 7. *Dog rose.* This is all the wild roses and includes the Alexander rose. They normally only flower for a short period but do form lovely hips.

They are only suitable for large gardens.

The planting and care of a rose garden demands a fair amount of thought and expertise. To help in choosing from the many varieties available, it is a good idea to consult a catalogue or to visit a rosarium. Roses must definitely stand in the sun, in fertile, light, chalky soil. They can be planted mid-October but make sure the ground is well dug. If roses have already been grown in the same piece of ground you will first have to clean all the worms from the soil or they will attack the new young roots. This can be done by digging out the soil to a depth of 80 cm and replacing it with fresh. Or, and this is a lot less work, by growing African marigolds in the same soil for a year. When planting, the part of the stem from which the shoots grow should be 5 cm above the ground. Bush roses, that is the hybrid teas and the floribundas, should be planted at 40 cm intervals. At the end of the season, build up the earth around the roses. You can use some of the earth between the bushes and pile it around the plants to protect the sensitive shoots from frost. The resultant holes can be filled with a mixture of garden compost and old manure. Except for climbing roses which are pruned in summer, pruning should take place in March and everything cut back to 10 or 15 cm above the ground. Good pruning is, however, an art so it is a good idea to get some tips before you begin. Dead flowers and suckers must be cut off.

SPIRAEA bumalda 'Anthony Waterer'
Spiraea

Flowering period: July to September.
Colour: crimson(flower), red(fully grown leaf).
Height: 50-100 cm.
The spiraea, with its masses of flowers, gives the
garden a lot of colour – red, pink or white.
The one shown here blooms the longest: right
through the summer. It makes few demands on the
soil, but should be planted in the full sun.
Because it flowers on the young wood, it is advisable
to cut it right back in the spring; this will also ensure
that if flowers fully. 'Anthony Waterer' is often used
as a hedge.

SPIRAEA vanhouttei
Spiraea

Flowering period: mid-May to mid-June.
Colour: white.
Height: up to 2 metres.
Because the spiraea is so strong and has such a
mass of flowers, no large garden should be without
one. Its many varieties mean that there is a place in
all gardens for this easy to grow deciduous shrub. To
ensure that it flowers fully, plant it in the full sun.
Otherwise the Spir. vanhouttei needs little attention.
As it is laden with blooms and has overhanging
branches, it is better to plant it on its own so that it
has plenty of space.

SYMPHORICARPOS albus 'White Hedge'
Snowberry

Flowering period: June to July.
Colour: pink(blossom), white(berry).
Height: 1 to 1.5 metres.
The snowberry is particularly suitable for a dark
corner of the garden: it grows in deep shade where
its white berries bring a touch of brightness. Because
birds do not eat the berries, these remain on the bush
from September to January. In autumn the leaves
turn yellow-red before they fall. As the name implies,
this one, with its dense growth and exceptional
sturdiness, can be used as a hedge. In addition, it
can be shaped to suit its surroundings.

SYRINGA vulgaris hybrid
Syringa

Flowering period: late May.
Colour: lilac, pink, white, purple.
Height: 3-5 metres.
The syringa, which comes from south-east Europe, is
a particularly popular deciduous shrub because of its
huge flowers. The most common is Syr. vulg., the
'common syringa', with its rich bloom. However, its
flowering period is short so consider planting one of
the early or late blooming varieties next to it so that
you have flowers for longer. Syringas need loamy,
well drained soil, full sun and extra fertiliser (i.e.
lime).

SYRINGA vulgaris hybrid
Syringa

Flowering period: late May.
Colour: white, lilac pink, purple.
Height: 3-5 metres.
A syringa has been developed in France specifically as a cutting flower. Grown in greenhouses, it is already in full bloom by the end of the year, and its fresh, sweet fragrance will dispel the musty winter atmosphere in any house. Garden syringas, too, provide excellent cutting flowers. To ensure it flowers fully, the shrub needs a lot of compost and lime. Limit pruning to the old wood, but cut off dead flowers at once.

TAMARIX tetrandra
Tamarisk

Flowering period: May to early June.
Colour: pale pink(flower), green-russet(branch).
Height: 3-5 metres.
Originally from dry, desert ares, the tamarisk needs a certain amount of salt to prevent it from drying out. It therefore does extremely well in coastal areas where the sea wind will not bother it at all. With its long, elegant branches it looks most attractive in park or garden, particularly in combination with conifers. However, it should not be planted next to largeleafed shrubs because it will disappear from view. Prune in July.

VIBURNUM burkwoodii
Viburnum

Flowering period: April.
Colour: pale pink(flower), green changing to red(leaf).
Height: 2-3 metres.
In 1924 the growers Burkwood and Skipwith of Kingston on Thames cultivated the Vib. burkwoodii by crossing Vib. carlesii with Vib. utile. It is a flimsy evergreen shrub with flowers that are not only very pretty but also have a gorgeous perfume, reminiscent of the freesia. It needs moist, fertile soil and full sun. It will also grow very well in the city.

VIBURNUM lantana
Wayfaring Tree

Flowering period: May to June.
Colour: yellow-white(flower), red to black(berry).
Height: 3-5 metres.
The Viburnum lantana is sometimes called the 'woolly snowball' because of its dense foliage and hundreds of tiny white flowers. Unlike the previous viburnum, the Vib. lantane is not an evergreen. It prefers dry, lime rich soil in the full sun. Like the tamarisk, it withstands both salt and wind making it very suitable as a windbreak in coastal areas. This Viburnum is poisonous.

VIBURNUM opulus 'Roseum'
Guelder Rose

Flowering period: May to June.
Colour: pale green to white(flower), green(summer leaf), red,(autumn leaf).
Height: 2-4 metres.
The guelder rose is the variety of Viburnum most often found growing wild. This Viburnum opulus 'Roseum' is sometimes called Viburnum opulus 'Sterile' because of its infertile flower. The shrub carries such a mass of flowers that its branches bend under the weight. It needs moist, fertile soil and a sunny spot.

VINCA minor
Lesser Periwinkle

Flowering period: May to September.
Colour: lilac-blue(flower).
Height: 20 cm.
Indigenous to Europe and Asia Minor, this is a popular and useful creeper. Its 4 cm long leaf is oval and a shiny dark green, and does not fall in autumn. It is not fussy about soil and will even flourish in the shade of trees or large shrubs. As soon as the shoots touch the earth they put down roots, which means that it rapidly propagates itself. Periwinkle blooms all through the summer and is extremely winter resistant.

WEIGELA 'Bristol Ruby'
Weigela

Flowering period: May to June.
Colour: crimson(flower), russet(branches).
Height: 2-3 metres.
Indigenous to Asia, the weigela is a deciduous shrub with beautiful deep red flowers. In principle, it will grow in all soils, but it flowers better in fertile, well drained earth.
It looks particularly nice when contrasted with jasmine and spiraea. Very winter resistant, it will do well in a city atmosphere. Because of the energy expended in flowering, it is recommended that the shrub is fertilised after it has bloomed.

WISTERIA sinensis
Wisteria

Flowering period: April to May.
Colour: violet-blue(flower).
Height: up to 6 metres(climber).
A native of East Asia, this is a very fast growing climber: some varieties are already 4 metres tall after two years. The flowers of the Wist. sinensis, which appear before the leaves form, are violet blue and grow in 10-20 cm long sprays.
For good growth it needs fertile soil and a sheltered spot in the full sun. It sheds its leaves in winter. Wisteria can be cut right back in summer; this encourages a fuller bloom.

CHAPTER 2

CONIFERS

Conifers are trees with needles, although the name 'coniferus' has nothing to do with the needles but with the fruit. Coniferus is Latin for 'cone bearing', something that most conifers do. The scales of the cone are the seeds with which the tree propagates itself.

Just about all conifers stay green in winter: the needle is actually a folded up leaf that withstands the cold of winter because such a small amount of its surface is exposed to the elements. For the same reason, a conifer also withstands heat! But there are one or two conifers that do shed their needles: the best known being the larch. The needles are usually shiny, although some are scaly like those of the cypress and juniper.

It is really not surprising that the interest in conifers has become so great over the years. There are so many varieties available from nurseries in such a huge number of shapes and colours that several suitable conifers can be found for every garden. They provide the stable, restful element so necessary as a basis for the other plants.

A conifer needs little care. Most of them should not be pruned or they lose their shape. However, some of the scaly conifers, i.e. the yew, can be pruned. Removing dead wood is something that must be done with all varieties.

Just about all conifers like well drained, sandy soil, even when just planted. More important, they should be kept well watered once planted. Until the roots have taken properly, there is a risk that the plant will dry out, because it continues to give out moisture through its needles before the roots are taking water from the soil.

If you transplant larger conifers you should bear this in mind, and it is advisable to protect the tree from the sun for a while with something like jute.

CHAMAECYPARIS
Dwarf or imitation cypress

Chamaecyparis only grows wild in Japan and in the north west of the United States where whole stretches of imitation cypresses form forests along the coast. The English name 'dwarf cypress' certainly does not apply to the wild varieties because some of these, such as the Chamaecyparis lawsoniana, reach 20-30 metres in height. However, these are not often grown in this country where nurseries provide a very large variety of the cultivated cypress in lots of shapes, sizes and colours. These are often the young tree kept small, and the fully mature trees are only used in very large gardens or parks. It is an evergreen conifer, usually conical, and with flat, scale-like needles that only become spikey when fully out. The ends of the branches droop slightly. Its fruit is small cones measuring 1 cm but these only appear after many years. Chamaecyparis is becoming more and more popular in British gardens, and no wonder. It makes a lovely background for the flowerbeds, particularly when several varieties are planted together in a group. In addition, imitation cypresses are very sturdy. They grow in all types of soil, as long as this is fertile and well drained. In this country they are winter resistant, and the only thing they will not withstand is a strong sea wind. So, if you live on the coast, you must plant them in a sheltered spot. Chamaecyparis can be propagated from seeds, cuttings or by rooting the long shoots directly into the earth. Among the Chamaecyparis lawsoniana are: 'Columnaris', pillar-shaped, 3-4 metres in 10-15 years, with grey green foliage. 'Ellwoodii', wider but slightly shorter, grey or blue-green. 'Kelleris Gold', pointed and conical with feathery yellow, later yellow-green, leaf, 1.5 to 2 metres in 10-15 years. 'Golden Wonder', another conical shape, the top and the ends of the branches droop slightly, deep golden yellow in colour. 'Minima Clauca', a small, first round, later conical shrub, that even after many years does not grow taller than one metre. Its colour is blue-green. 'Stewartii', with drooping top and boughs, is golden yellow in summer, yellow-green in winter. Gonical, it reaches 1.5 to 2 metres in 10-15 years. 'Clauca Spek', grows to the same height as the previous one, either conical or in pillar shape, with grey-blue needles.

'Tharandtensis Caesia' is a round, later broad and conical dwarf shrub with frosty blue needles. Of the Japanese Chamaecyparis pisifera: 'Boulevard', a dwarf tree that grows to just 1.20 metres in 10-15 years. It has a regular pyramid shape and silver-blue, later grey-blue needles. 'Filifera Nana', a round dwarf shrub that, because of its long threadlike branches, looks like a green mop. 'Filifera Aurea Nana', as tall as its broad, it is a golden yellow bush with threadlike, drooping branches. After 10-15 years it is still only one metre tall. 'Filifera Sungold', grows low and broad over the ground with yellow-green threadlike branches. 'Squarrosa', a medium height tree with an irregular pyramid form, silver grey in colur. 'Plumosa', a broad conical tree, 3-4 metres in 10-15 years. The dark green needles grow very close together. Chamaecyparis nootkatensis 'Pendula', with its wide and spacious boughs, resembles a cedar or spruce. Its smaller branches hang straight downwards from the main boughs. It is dark green, and reaches 3-4 metres in 10-15 years. Chamaecyparis nootkatensis 'Glauca' is a thin, pyramid-shaped tree, 3-5 metre in 10-15 years, blue-green in colour. Chamaecyparis obtusa 'Nana Gracilis' has shell-shaped, curved ends to its smaller branches. It grows very slowly to a height of 2 metres, and later becomes conical. It is shiny dark green.

ARAUCARIA araucana
Snake Fir or Monkey Tree

Flowering period: insignificant.
Colour: dark green.
Height: 3-5 metres in 10-15 years.
The scientific name of the monkey tree is taken from the Arauca indians of Chile, from whose area it comes. It has an absolutely straight trunk with horizontal, well-spaced, snake-like branches. Its strange shape is due to the fact that the wide, triangular, spikey needles, which also cover the trunk, grow in layers over each other, like the scales of a fish. This tree likes sea air and slightly acid, humus rich soil.
It is not completely winter resistant.

CEDRUS atlantica 'Glauca'
Atlas Cedar

Flowering period: insignificant.
Colour: bluish white(needles).
Height: 20 metres.
Cedars like dry, well drained, lime rich soil. This, of course, includes the atlas cedar which comes from the dry forests of the North African Atlas mountains. It grows into a pyramid shape with widely spaced, rather irregular branches.
Because of this it shows to best advantage when it stands alone, e.g. in the middle of large lawn. The needles, which are 2 cm long, grow in small clumps. It can withstand frost and dryness but not too much wind.

CEDRUS deodara
Himalayan Cedar

Flowering period: insignificant.
Colour: dark bluish green(needles).
Height: 15 metres.
Just like all cedars this one, too, needs well-drained, dry soil. But unlike the Atlas cedar, this one does not like lime. It grows in pyramid form, and the small branches hang like pendants from the horizontal main branches. The cones are 8-12 cm long, and the dark bluish green needles 2.5 to 5 cm. It shows to best advantage when it stands alone, but it must be protected from the wind. Frost and dryness are not a problem.

CHAMAECÝPARIS lawsoniana 'Alumii'
Dwarf Cypress

Flowering period: insignificant.
Colour: bluish green(needles).
Height: 3-4 metres in 10-15 years.
This evergreen tree adapts well to varying circumstances. With the exception of sand or clay, it will grow in any type of soil. To begin with it grows in the form of a pillar but later it bushes out from underneath. Because it is a fast grower it is often planted in hedges. The only thing that it absolutely cannot withstand is sea wind.

CHAMAECÝPARIS lawsoniona 'Golden Wonder'
Dwarf Cypress

Flowering period: insignificant.
Colour: deep golden yellow(needles).
Height: 150 cm in 10-15 years.
This is not a fast growing tree, although when mature it can reach 6 metres. It grows in a very even pyramid shape with fan like branches. It withstands frost but does not like sea wind. It makes no special demands on the soil, which can be acid or lime rich, dry or damp. The needles are broad and scale-shaped and hardly change in colour the whole year.

CHAMAECÝPARIS pisifera 'Filifera Aurea'
Dwarf Cypress

Flowering period: insignificant.
Colour: golden yellow(needles).
Height: 80-100 cm in 10-15 years.
This is a real dwarf cypress, a rather round bush, which grows at the same rate in both height and breadth. The thread-like, overhanging branches have broad, scale-shaped needles. It keeps its needles in winter and they do not change colour. The soil can be either acid or rich in lime. It does not withstand sea wind very well, so in gardens on the coast it must be protected.

JUNIPERUS communis 'Suecia'
Juniper

Flowering period: insignificant.
Colour: grey blue(needles).
Height: 150-250 cm in 10-15 years.
This cultivated variety of the juniper grows in the shape of a pillar which means, of course, that its branches grow straight upwards. A fully mature tree can reach 5 and sometimes 6 metres in height. It is a sturdy conifer that does well in all types of soil, whether this is acid or rich in lime. The needles are long and prickly, usually grey blue in colour but in poor soil they will be silvery. It does not lose its needles in winter.

JUNIPERUS squamata 'Blue Carpet'
Juniper

Flowering period: insignificant.
Colour: bluish green(needles), dark blue(berries).
Height: 30 cm tall, by 1.5 to 2 metres wide.
With the name 'Blue Carpet', it is no surprise that this is a coniferous creeper. It is very suitable for flowerbeds, heather and rock gardens and makes few demands of the soil or climate. In the Netherlands the berries are used as flavouring for jenever (a sort of gin), while the oil from the berries and wood is medicinal. The wood is used for making pencils and other things. If you cut into the stem you will smell the fragrance.

54

JUNIPERUS
Juniper

The juniper belongs to the cypress family. It is an evergreen conifer with needle-like foliage and round, fleshy berries. It was once highly prized for its medicinal qualities and, as often happens with medicinal plants, it was the subject of mysterious stories. These days the oil from the wood of the juniper is only used in homeopathy. One or two juniper branches on the fire when grilling or smoking meat or fish add a delicious aroma to these dishes. And, of course, the berries have been used for years in the distilling of jenever and gin; and everyone who has eaten sauerkraut will recognise their taste because they are used in the flavouring. The common juniper, Juniperus communis, is indigenous to this country, and also to other European countries, North America, Asia and Africa. It grows very slowly, probably because of the poor soil in which it grows wild, but can eventually reach 10 or 15 metres. The reddish brown wood of the juniper is tough and durable. Amongst other things it is used for making matches and walking sticks. Older trees can be recognised by their peeling bark. The needles are rather stiff, ending in a sharp point. Its bloom is not spectacular, with tiny yellow (male) and green (female) flowers. The dark berries take two years in which to ripen. Junipers are very sturdy, making them suitable for a great many situations. Cold, heat and dryness will not harm them. They also make no special demands on the soil, which can be either acid or very rich in loam. The common juniper can be propagated from the seed that forms after the second year, and many can be grown from cuttings. Some of the lovely hybrids of Juniperus communis are: 'Suecia', pillar shaped with greyish blue, in poor soil silver, needles. 1.5 to 2.5 metres tall in 10-15 years. 'Hibernica' forms a slightly thinner pillar than the previous one, stays smaller and has bluish green, blunt needles. 'Repanda' is a slow growing dense creeper, 50 cm tall and 2 metres wide when fully grown. The needles are dark green with a silver stripe. 'Hornibrookii' is also a slow growing creeper but with lighter coloured, sharp needles. Of the Juniperus chinensis: 'Keteleerii', pillar or slim conical shape with blue scaly needles and a lovely fragrence. It reaches 1.5 to 2 metres in 10-15 years

and bears a mass of blue berries. 'Hetzii', a large shrub with a short trunk and funnel shaped, wide spreading main branches, 2-3 metres tall and wide in 10-15 years. The scaly needles are greyish blue. 'Plumosa Aurea' is a dwarf shrub that grows to 1 metre in 10-15 years. It is very bushy with an irregular funnel shape and golden yellow, later yellow-green, scaly needles. The Juniperus horizontalis 'Glauca' is an excellent creeper that forms a dense grey-blue carpet. Juniperus squamata 'Meyeri' is a heavily branched, up to 1.5 metres tall bush with a lovely bluish grey colour. Very special is the Juniperus virginiana 'Skyrocket', the thinnest conifer in the world. At 2 metres tall it is only 30 cm wide. It can reach 6 to 8 metres and has blue-green needles.

JUNIPERUS virginiana 'Skyrocket'
Juniper

Flowering period: insignificant.
Colour: bluish green(needles).
Height: 3-4 metres after 10-15 years, to a max. 9 m.
The 'Skyrocket' ist the thinnest of the conifers. The juniper family therefore contains not only creeping conifers but also one that looks like a rocket. And there are many more varieties, in all shapes and sizes. So it is no wonder that the juniper – that makes few demands, comes in so many shapes, gives medicinal oil and also looks attractive – is one of the most popular of all the conifers.

LARIX kaempferi
Japanese Larch

Flowering period: April.
Colour: bluish green(needles), yellow(flowers).
Height: 25 metres.
This larch grows faster than others of its family and can take a certain amount of dryness. Because of this it is more popular than the European larch. It has a continuous straight trunk, and because the branches grow upwards, its crown is shaped rather like a pyramid. It loses its needles in winter, and in the autumn it is golden yellow. It grows best in a heavy loam soil, or in well-drained earth rich in humus.

PICEA abies 'Ohlendorfii'
Spruce

Flowering period: insignificant.
Colour: pale green(needles).
Height: 2-3 metres.
This is one of the many cultivated varieties of the spruce or Christmas tree. It grows in the shape of a wide pyramid, and because of its low height it is very suitable for small garden. It grows best in light, cool, clayey soil with lime. But it also flourishes in loam, sandy loam or sand. Naturally it withstands winter weather when, just like other spruce, it does not shed its needles.

PICEA pungens 'Glauca Globosa'
Colorado Spruce

Flowering period: insignificant.
Colour: silver blue(needles).
Height: 80-100 cm in 10-15 years.
This conifer is a dwarf version of the blue spruce or Colorado spruce. Its early growth is loose and irregular, but later it forms a tight, very conical shape. The needles grow very close together and measure 12 mm in length. It likes a light, cool clay, loam or sandy soil with lime.
It will withstand smoke or small amounts of salt, and is not affected by a harsh winter.

PINUS mugo var. mughus
Fir

Flowering period: insignificant.
Colour: dark green(needles).
Height: 80-100 cm in 10-15 years.
This fir comes from the Balkans and the eastern part of the Alps. Although most firs are proper trees, this one grows like a bush: wide and not higher than two or three metres even in maturity.
The 4 cm long needles grow close together in pairs, and are often curved. It likes soils rich in humus or minerals, which can be damp to rather dry, with acid or a little lime. What is essential is light.

PINUS nigra var. nigra
Austrian Fir or Black Fir

Flowering period: insignificant.
Colour: dark green(needles).
Height: 30 metres.
This type of black fir grows quickly and after ten years is already too big for the small garden.
It is an extremely sturdy tree which makes it very important in forestry. It can be planted in areas where the coarse fir will not grow, because this black fir makes virtually no demands on either the soil or the climate. It withstands frost, smoke, wind, heat and dryness. Its needles are 9-16 cm long.

PINUS sylvestris 'Watereri'
Fir

Flowering period: insignificant.
Colour: bluish green(needles).
Height: 80-100 cm in 10-15 years.
This is a fir that grows like a shrub. At first it grows straight upwards, but later it bushes out and becomes conical or even round. Even when fully mature it seldom reaches more than 2 m. The needles are 4 cm long, stiff, slightly curved and grow close together. In dry soil it has a silver blue colour. It prefers a very dry to slightly damp spot, and the soil can be from acid to very rich in lime. Dryness does not affect it.

PSEUDOLARIX amabilis
Golden Larch

Flowering period: insignificant.
Colour: bright green(needles).
Height: 10 metres.
This larch is a native of South-East China. It is a tree with horizontal branches with very bushy growth. Because of this, it is better if it stands alone, e.g. on a lawn. It differs from other larches in that the scales of its cones open wide. In the autumn, before it loses its needles, it has a golden yellow colour. These needles are thin and soft and grow together in bunches. It prefers fertile soil with very little lime.

PINUS
Fir or pine

Just like the spruce, the fir is very important in forestry. It grows quickly and gives good wood from which resin and terpentine can also be extracted. In addition, it is often planted in mountainous regions to overcome the problem of soil erosion. It is an extremely strong tree with excellent resistance to cold, heat and dryness. It is easy to distinguish from the spruce by its needles. Those of the fir are generally longer and grow in groups, with 2, 3, 5 or 7 bunches together. It belongs with the conifers that remain green in winter. Most firs are trees, but there

are also one or two shrubs, and they are indigenous to Europe, Asia and America. The cones ripen in autumn one, and sometimes two, years after the tree has bloomed. You can plant the wild varieties as long as you have a very large garden. Otherwise, you are recommended to grow the cultivated forms, of which there is a great number available from nurseries. Amongst these are also a number of dwarf varieties that look lovely in a rock garden. In general, firs prefer a light spot and airy, well drained soil. The wild varieties of Pinus can be raised easily from

seed, whilst the cultivated forms are grown from cuttings. One of the varieties that grows wild in this country is the Pinus sylvestris, the coarse pine. It was originally indigenous to Britain, but the lack of any genuine forests means that they have been specially planted. It makes virtually no demands on its environment and will grow anywhere. It usually has an extremely straight trunk, but in windy areas you will see it bent into all sorts of fantastic shapes. Pinus aristata, from the high mountains of the Sierra Nevada, is a low growing shrublike pine with a curly shape and dark or bluish green needles. The Pinus cembra, with its bushy growth, comes from the mountains of Central and Eastern Europe and reaches a height of 25 metres. However, in a garden it has a thin, conical shape and seldom grows taller than 5 metres. Its 10 cm long needles are bluish green. Pinus contorta, from North America, is a small, conical tree. Its curved, 5 cm long needles are bright green and form in pairs. It reaches 2-3 metres in 10-15 years. Pinus leucodermis, from the Balkan, reaches the same height. This one is densely branched with a broad, conical crown.

The stiff, 8 cm long, upright needles are dark green. Pinus mugo, from the mountains of Central and Southern Europe, is a bush pine that grows to 1.5 to 2.5 metres in 10-15 years. It is sometimes a thin, conical shape, but more often grows into a broad shrub. It has curved, dark green, 4 cm long needles. Pinus mugo var. mughus from the Balkans, is the smallest of this family. It has a more bushy growth but reaches just 80-100 cm in 10-15 years. Pinus nigra, from the mountain forests of South-Eastern Europe, is a tall tree with a broad, conical crown and long, dark green needles. An extremely sturdy tree, it is certainly not suitable for smaller gardens. Pinus peuce, the Macedonian pine, of of average height with grey-green needles. It reaches 2-3 metres in 10-15 years. Its branches begin from the ground and its crown is broad and loose. Sadly,

Pinus pinea, the lovely parasol of a tree found all around the coast of the Mediterranean Sea, is not resistant to our winter climate. Some of the good cultivated varieties are: Pinus strobus 'Radiata', a bluish green dwarf, only 1 metre tall after 15 years. Pinus silvestris 'Watereri', a shrub, also bluish green but with shorter, curved needles. Pinus silvestris 'Fastigiata' which grows into a pillar with steel blue, 6 cm long needles. It reaches 3-4 metres in 10-15 years. Pinus parviflora 'Glauca' is a small, capricious fir with lovely curved silver-blue needles. Pinus mugo 'Gnom' and Pinus mugo 'Mops' are dark green dwarf firs very suitable for rock gardens.

TAXUS baccata 'Dovastonii Aurea'
Yew

Flowering period: insignificant.
Colour: yellow green(needles), red(fruit).
Height: 120-150 cm in 10-15 years.
This is a small tree or shrub with horizontal branches which overhang only at the top, where the extreme ends hang downwards. In winter the needles turn golden brown but do not fall. In September it bears striking red, fleshy fruit. The seeds and the green parts of the plant are poisonous. It grows to best advantage when it stands alone in moist soil, which can be slightly acid to very richt in lime.

TAXUS baccata 'Fastigiata'
Yew

Flowering period: insignificant.
Colour: very dark green(needles), red(fruit).
Height: 80-120 cm in 10-15 years.
This nursery variety of the taxus grows in the shape of a pillar. From the ground it forms increasing numbers of branches, which, like the smaller branches, grow straight upwards. Mature trees can reach 3-5 m. The 3 cm long needles point in all directions and bend downwards. In September it puts forth striking red, fleshy fruit measuring 1 cm across. The seeds and the green parts of the plant are very poisonous. It prefers moist, slightly acid soil.

THUJA occidentalis 'Little Champion'
Cedar

Flowering period: insignificant.
Colour: green(needles).
Height: up to 80 cm.
There is really just one thing necessary for growing the cedar, and that is well drained soil.
Like most other conifers, it is an evergreen. Because of its dense foliage it is often used as a hedge. Although this is not the case with the one shown here, which is a dwarf. It is a very round shrub, generally planted alone or between other low plants. It looks particularly nice in a heather garden.

THUJA occidentalis 'Pyramidalis Compacta'
Cedar

Flowering period: insignificant.
Colour: bright green(needles).
Height: 12 metres.
As its name implies, this cultivated variety of the Thuja is pyramid-shaped. It is a very common tree, but if raised from seed it may not grow in exactly the right shape. The branches and myriad twigs are covered with scale like 'needles' which grow up to 4 mm in length. The undersides of these produce resin. The Thuja does well in all types of soil, as long as this is moist and light. It will withstand winter weather very well, but hates cats' urine.

CHAPTER 3
TREES

In the introduction you will have read that the tree has a special place in the plant world. The space given in this guide is far too limited and the following pages contain only about twenty trees. But, for many gardens, a tree is too big and, however much we would like to, we cannot find room for the majority of them in a small town garden. Even so, those covered in this chapter are not the smallest, because we did not want to omit the better known foliates – and some of these are very large. Often, though, the well known large trees can be found in smaller sizes. For instance, there is a low, drooping variety of the birch available (Betula verrucosa 'Youngii'), the creeping willow (Salix repens) and the Robinia pseudoacacia 'Tortuosa', a low, curly Robinia.

The Italian poplar, which is pillar shaped, can be made suitable for a smaller garden by topping it when it reaches about 3 metres in height: you cut out the top and the tree then only grows in width. There is a small variety of alder (Alnus incana 'Aurea') that grows no taller than 6 metres. There is also the Sorbus vilmorinii, a mountain ash, which reaches about the same height. The Maythorn is a somewhat larger tree but does have the advantage that it can be pruned into any shape. This shrub-like Maythorn is therefore also suitable as a hedge.

Finally, the Rhus typhina grows no higher than 5 metres and is very pretty with its large, upright plumes.

All in all, there is a reasonable number of trees for the small garden that will give it a special atmosphere. In general, foliates need little attention. Take out the dead wood and prune only as much as is necessary for the shape you want. Information about planting and transplanting can be found in the general introduction under deciduous trees.

ACER platanoides
Norwegian Maple

Flowering period: April.
Colour: yellow-green(flower), green(leaf).
Height: up to 30 metres.
Despite its English name, this huge tree is not from Northern Europe, but from Central and Southern Europe. It is too large for the average garden and is usually found in parks and along streets. The long, 10-18 cm wide leaf has five sharply pointed segments. Like all maples – there are about 150 varieties – its leaves turn yellow before falling in winter. It prefers fertile, lime rich soil.

AESCULUS hippocastanum
White Horse Chestnut

Flowering period: May to June.
Colour: white(flower), green(leaf).
Height: 25 metres.
This is the most common chestnut in Britain and also the only one indigenous to Europe. It is found growing wild in Bulgaria and Northern Greece. In earlier times it was thought that the chestnuts from this tree could cure horses of a cough, hence the name horse chestnut. It has long, pointed, hand like groups of leaves, and blooms with 30 cm long upright plumes. It is only suitable for very large gardens.

ALNUS incana
White or Grey Alder

Flowering period: March.
Colour: dark green(leaf).
Height: 20 metres.
This grows wild not only in Europe but also in America and Asia. It has a pyramid-shaped crown and grey bark, giving it a strong resemblance to Alnus glutinosa, the black alder. The leaf is oval, pointed and double serrated, with a light greyish-green, hairy underside. The caracteristic catkins, the male form of the flower, are longer than those of the grey alder. It flourishes in moist or dry soil.

BETULA verrucosa
Sand Birch

Flowering period: April to May.
Colour: bright green(leaf), white(bark).
Height: 20-25 metres.
Also indigenous to Britain, this birch is known as rough or hard. And no wonder considering that the peeling bark is like sandpaper to the touch.
It is a light wood, meaning that it prefers to stand in the sun. The triangular, coarsely serrated leaf turns golden yellow in autumn.
Although bare in winter, its white bark and lovely shape keep it attractive. It grows in all soils.

BETULA verrucosa 'Youngii'
Birch

Flowering period: insignificant.
Colour: summer green.
Height: average.
This is one of the lovely 'weeping' types of rough birch that are very popular. Unlike others of this type which are more suitable for open country, this is a real garden tree. It has a split trunk, a round crown and branches that bend to the ground. Its leaf differs little from other birch. It grows in all soils but, because of its shallow root system, takes a lot of goodness from the lawn or flowerbed.

CASTANEA sativa
Sweet Chestnut

Flowering period: May to June.
Colour: dark green and shiny(leaf).
Height: 20 metres.
Roasted chestnuts are a delicacy. In Paris they are sold on every street corner in autumn. This generous tree is a wide branched giant with a shield shaped crown, and is certainly not suitable for the average garden. It is indigenous to Southern Europe, Asia Minor and North Africa.
It blooms with rather unspectacular yellow-white catkins, and the main attraction is its huge, coarsely serrated, shiny leaves. It does not mind shade, and likes fertile, moist soil.

CRATAEGUS carrierei
Hawthorn

Flowering period: May.
Colour: white with pink centre(flower).
Height: 7 metres.
This is one of the lovely hawthorn hybrids. An erratic tree with thorny branches, its green summer leaf is oval, serrated and 5-10 cm long.
In autumn it puts forth orange-red, pear-shaped fruit of nearly 2 cm in length. This keeps it colourful until well into winter and also attracts many birds.
Because it stays small and blooms richly in spring, it is a lovely tree for the garden. It prefers light, lime rich soil.

FAGUS sylvatica 'Atropurpurea'
Beech

Flowering period: insiginificant.
Colour: purple(leaf).
Height: 30 metres.
The stately beech is ideal for our climate, liking as it does moderate winters, cool summers and lots of rain. Easy to recognise amongst other trees because of its shiny trunk, it is always to be found in old parks and along old roads. The many tiny oval leaves give it a wide crown. Beech cast so much shadow that no other plants will grow underneath them. Even so, beech woods are not as sombre as, for example, pine woods.

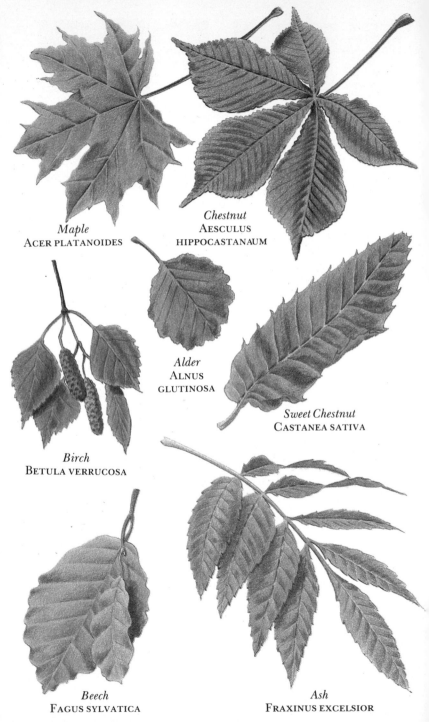

Maple
ACER PLATANOIDES

Chestnut
AESCULUS
HIPPOCASTANAUM

Alder
ALNUS
GLUTINOSA

Birch
BETULA VERRUCOSA

Sweet Chestnut
CASTANEA SATIVA

Beech
FAGUS SYLVATICA

Ash
FRAXINUS EXCELSIOR

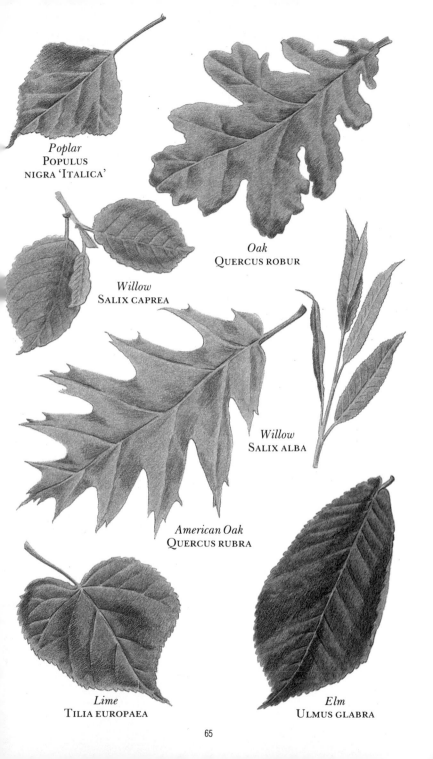

Poplar
POPULUS
NIGRA 'ITALICA'

Oak
QUERCUS ROBUR

Willow
SALIX CAPREA

Willow
SALIX ALBA

American Oak
QUERCUS RUBRA

Lime
TILIA EUROPAEA

Elm
ULMUS GLABRA

FRAXINUS excelsior
Ash

Flowering period: May (unspectacular).
Colour: bright green(leaf).
Height: 30-40 metres.
There are 60 types of ash, of which half come from
America and the rest from Europe and Asia.
Fraxinus excelsior is the common ash and has the
tickest foliage of all our trees. In autumn the long
feathery leaf turns yellow.
The young tree will grow well in shade, but once
mature it must stand in the full sun. It prefers moist,
fertile and lime rich soil. Ash wood is durable and
flexible.

PLATANUS acerifolia
Plane Tree

Flowering period: May (unspectacular).
Colour: summer green(leaf).
Height: 30 metres.
When you sit on a terrace on a well shaded square in
the South of France in summer, nine times out of ten
it is the plane tree that provides that shade. The
origin of Platanus acerifolia is not known, but it
appears to be a hybrid of the American Platanus
occidentalis and the European Platanus orientalis.
It has the characteristics of the plane tree: shiny,
dappled bark and long, pointed leaf with 3-5
segments that resembles that of the maple.

POPULUS nigra 'Italica'
Poplar

Flowering period: insignificant.
Colour: bright green(leaf).
Height: a tall tree.
Poplars are famous for their speed of growth. That is
why they are important to trade and industry. In
addition, the poplar is a pioneer, preparing the
ground for other types of wood that will not grow in
virgin soil. It is often found in newly built areas where
it quickly puts paid to the initial bareness. This one
grows into a pillar shape, with branches from the
ground up, and is often used as a windbreak. .

POPULUS tremula
Aspen

Flowering period: April.
Colour: bright green(leaf).
Height: 20 metres.
The 3-8 cm long, almost circular leaves on their flat
stems are set in motion by the slightest breath of
wind. Hence the saying 'to quiver like an aspen' It is
a native of this country and is characterised by its
loose, translucent crown and light, shiny bark. Like
other poplars it grows quickly in all soils, which it
also prepares for other trees. It is not suitable for
roadsides because of its thick, bunchy roots, but is
used for making paper and matches.

QUERCUS robur
Summer Oak

Flowering period: insignificant.
Colour: bright green(leaf).
Height: 20-30 metres.
Old oaks are huge, strong trees with thick trunks and heavy, gnarled branches. This old giant stirs the imagination, particularly when standing alone in a field. The summer oak is the most common in the British landscape. The bark shines initially and only begins to show deep, vertical cracks after 15 years. The budding leaf is russet with irregular segments and a very short stalk.

QUERCUS rubra
American Oak

Flowering period: insignificant.
Colour: dark green(leaf).
Height: 30 metres.
Given enough room, this too becomes a giant of a tree with a wide, round crown. The leaf differs from that of the summer oak in that it is more deeply serrated and the segments are pointed. In autumn it turns a lovely orange-red and is often used in bouquets. The young tree does better in shade than other oaks. The soil must not contain lime but need not be particularly rich or moist.

RHUS typhina
Stag's-horn Sumach

Flowering period: June to July.
Colour: crimson(flower), summer green(leaf).
Height: 5 metres.
A number of Rhus are extremely poisonous, but you can happily grow this one from the eastern part of the United States in your garden. It is not only safe, but also a decorative little tree with a wide, flat crown. The feathery leaf is at least 50 cm long, consists of 6–15 oblong smaller leaves, and turns a lovely orange-red in autumn. The leaves and the upright purple-red fruit holders are its most attractive features.

ROBINIA pseudoacacia
Imitation Acacia

Flowering period: June.
Colour: white(flower), fresh green(leaf).
Height: 25 metres.
Imitation, because the genuine acacia belongs to the Mimosaceae family. But with its groups of feathery leaves and thorny, angular boughs it looks like an acacia. It has a loose crown and a short thick trunk with deeply etched cracks. The long sprays of tiny, heavily perfumed butterfly flowers attract masses of bees. As long as it stands in the full sun it will grow in the driest and poorest of sandy soils. It is also a good soil preparer for other trees.

SALIX
Willow

The Salix family is found in all moderate climates. There are at least 300 varieties, from 1 metre tall shrubs to 25 metre tall trees. Most of them are found in moist soil, but a number of them will also grow well in dry ground. For instance, the Salix repens, the creeping willow, often grown in dunes to keep the sand together.

The best known is probably the pollard willow, which is not a variety but a name given because the shape of the willow is achieved by polling – the crown of the tree is cut off to produce a close head of young shoots. Originally polling was done for practical reasons. Farmers used the twigs for fencing and for propagating the tree.

These days, however, the practical reasons have disappeared and farmers leave the willow to grow out. But to preserve the well loved pollard willow for the landscape, volunteers have now taken over the polling. Most pollards are in fact the Salix alba, which is a tree that can reach 25 metres in height. It blooms with catkins in April and its only demand on the soil is for the moistness mentioned earlier. It is suitable as a windbreak, for strengthening embankments and as a pollard on farm estates and along ditches.

A beautiful willow is the Salix alba 'Tristis' the weeping willow. This is often found in parks and public gardens. Besides the large willows, there are also the smaller ones like the previously mentioned creeping willow, that grows just 1 to 1.5 metres tall. The most common small willow is the water willow (Salix caprea), a shrub that bears striking thick yellow catkins in March or April. Because this is a cultivated male plant, it will not propagate itself. It is often found in parks and gardens. The Salix caprea 'Pendula' is a low growing weeping tree with silver grey catkins. It is grafted onto another stem and its height is therefore dependent of the height of its host. A very special willow is the Salix matsudana 'Tortuosa', the curly willow, with its twisty branches and yellowy colour. It keeps its corkscrew boughs longer if pruned, and can reach 7 metres without losing its special appearance.

Willow wood, particularly from Salix alba, is still used for making clogs in the Netherlands because it is strong, supple and virtually water proof. The Dutch also use the thinner twigs for making a sort of mattress for use in dike building and for strengthening embankments.

SALIX alba 'Tristis'
Weeping Willow

Flowering period: April (unspectacular).
Colour: sea green(leaf).
Height: 15-20 metres.
Like all willows, the weeping willow likes low lying, moist soil. Not surprising then that it grows well in parts of Britain. The very wide, bell-shaped crown is formed from horizontal boughs and thin, yellow branches that droop to the ground. The leaf is thin and pointed. It is mainly found in parks, by ponds or lakes, with its branches hanging into the water. It prefers a sunny spot and is too large for the average garden.

SORBUS aucuparia
Mountain Ash

Flowering period: May.
Colour: white(flower), orange-red(fruit).
Height: up to 15 metres.
This is the common mountain ash, indigenous to Europe and Asia Minor and frequently found in parks, gardens and along lanes. It is easy to recognise by its feathery sprays of tiny, pointed and serrated leaves. Its most attractive feature is the bunches of brightly coloured berries that appear in late summer. These are a great delicacy to many birds. It likes acid soil and does not mind shade.

TILIA europaea
Dutch Lime

Flowering period: late June.
Colour: summer green(leaf).
Height: up to 40 metres.
There are some 30 different known varieties of the Tilia, most of which come from northern or central areas. The Dutch lime is a hybrid of Til. cordata and Til. platyphyllos. It is a huge park or street tree with a conical crown. The leaves are an irregular heart shape, pointed and sharply serrated. They bloom with long, pendulous sprays of flowers, that attract masses of bees (lime blossom honey).

ULMUS hollandica
Elm

Flowering period: early spring (unremarkable).
Colour: summer green(leaf).
Height: 35-40 metres.
These stately trees with their straight trunks and tick upright branches used to be very common in parks and along streets. But Dutch elm disease, the Ceratocystus fungus that attacks their bark, has rather decimated their numbers. They have a wide crown with two rows of alternated, single, oval and pointed leaves. Elms prefer fertile, drained soil.

CHAPTER 4

FRUIT IN THE GARDEN

As white rice and bread becomes rather less popular, so the interest in 'useful' plants grows – as if there could be plants without a use. Gradually, the ornamental maize is exchanged for one that is edible, the purely decorative cherry for one with some flavour, the pretty berry for the currant, and so on. And why not? An edible plant is often attractive in its own right, and it is really rather a strange idea to have any division between decorative and 'useful' plants at all.

However, we do make this distinction in this guide because fruit trees and shrubs need more attention than those that do not bear fruit. Perhaps this is why the change over has occured! Whatever the case may be, there is a lot of pleasure to be had from home grown fruit, and the care given to these plants does not have to be of a professional standard.

Whilst you cannot expect the same results, you do not have to work as hard. But even the professional grower does not have so much to do these days. One of the most difficult things about growing fruit is the fight against disease and pests. But if you buy a well cared for tree from a recognised nursery, the chance of disease is very small. Usually only approved trees are sold in nurseries and garden centres.

Unfortunately, there is not enough space in this guide to allow us to go into the pruning and treatment of pests for fruit plants. If you decide to buy a fruit tree or shrub, the nurseryman can give you information about this. As far as when to plant is concerned, most fruit trees and shrubs are planted in winter, except:

– blueberry, cherry, quince, medlar and fig, which should be planted in spring or autumn.

– grape and kiwi, which are planted in May.

– apricot, peach, plum and pear, which are planted in November.

Information on how to plant and transplant is in the general introduction. By reading the text in this chapter you will be able to decide which fruit suits you and your garden.

ACTINIDIA chinensis
Kiwi

Flowering period: May.
Colour: white(blossom), green-brown(fruit).
Height: up to 2 metres(climber).
Before enthusiasm runs away with you: this plant cannot be grown outdoors in this country, at least not for its fruit. But it does look nice creeping around pergolas or along walls. Only if it is an exceptional summer will the fruit form, and even then it will not ripen enough to be edible. The plant bears flowers of one sex, so you will need a male and a female plant if you still want to give the fruit a try.

CASTANEA sativa
Sweet Chestnut

Flowering period: May.
Colour: white(blossom), green(summer leaf), golden brown(autumn leaf), yellow-green(fruit).
Height: 20-30 metres.
Despite the fact that the sweet chestnut is very well known here, it actually comes from the Middle East and North Africa. It is a very sturdy tree that grows quickly in well drained, fertile and acid soil. Even after just a few years, it gives a reasonable yield of chestnuts. The leaves are thin, long and sharply serrated, and the blossom has a nice perfume. It should be planted where it will have plenty of space.

CORYLUS avellana
Hazel

Flowering period: February to March.
Colour: golden yellow(catkin), brown(fruit).
Height: up to 5 metres.
The hazel is really a shrub since it grows from the ground with several stems. It is deciduous and frost resistant and makes few demands on the soil – just that this must be well drained. It bears fruit if (cross) pollinated, so for the best results you should plant several different types of hazel together. It is often planted beneath larger plants because it flowers just as well in shade as in sun.

HIPPOPHAE rhamnoides
Sea Buckthorn

Flowering period: March to April.
Colour: orange(berry), dark green(leaf).
Height: up to 3.5 metres.
Sea buckthorn, as the name perhaps implies, prefers sandy soil and withstands salt and dryness, and is therefore very suitable for growing amongst dunes. The berries are extremely good for making jams and drinks because they are rich in vitamin C, but these will only form if there is a male and a female plant growing together. The shrub needs sandy, lime rich soil; and grows much more fully in the sun.

JUGLANS regia
Walnut

Flowering period: late May to early June.
Colour: green(leaf), light brown(fruit).
Height: up to 30 metres.
The mighty walnut with its broad crown and silver grey heavy boughs is indigenous to North Asia. The leaves appear fairly late, in June, when it also blooms. The flower is not particularly attractive but is important because it preceeds the fruit; a 20 year old tree yields the same number of kilos in nuts! The walnut thrives in heavy, well drained, fertile, lime rich soil with minerals, and should stand in the full sun.

MALUS sylvestris
Golden Renet

Flowering period: May.
Colour: pale pink(blossom), russet(fruit).
Height: 2-4 metres.
The golden renet has been one of the popular storage apples for some time. It is a tasty eater but is also used for cooking. To obtain the fruit the blossom must be cross pollinated with, for example, Cox, James Grieve or Laxton. The tree makes few demands on the soil and grows in just about any ground, but does need a sunny spot. Prune – as little as possible – in the second half of January.

MALUS sylvestris
Summer Red

Flowering period: April to May.
Colour: pale pink(blossom), dark red(fruit).
Height: 2-4 metres.
Unlike the golden renet, the summer red is a new variety and not yet very well known. Growers are constantly looking for improved varieties with better flavour, durability, appearance and resistance to diseases. The summer red is a lovely, very tasty eating apple. It blooms early so the apples are ready for picking by the end of August. James Grieve and Discovery are suitable for cross pollination with this one. Sunny and (frost) sheltered spot.

MESPILUS germanica
Medlar

Flowering period: May to June.
Colour: white(flower), brown-green(fruit), russet(autumn leaf).
Height: 4,5-9 metres.
If you were said to be 'as rotten as a medlar' it would be a compliment, because the fruit of this tree is at its most delicious when decayed. But the fruit is seldom seen, which is not surprising since it is very messy to eat. However, the medlar is worth growing for its huge flowers and deep red leaves. It makes few special demands.

MALUS
Apple

The apple is at least as old as Eve and ever since she tempted Adam with one, many women (amongst them the Greek goddes Aphrodite and Snow White's evil stepmother) have followed her example. The innocent looking apple has gained a treacherous reputation from all this. And certainly the Granny Smith is a 'poisonous' green! But before the Granny Smith existed, there had been countless inferior apples. Even today wild apples can be found in some parts of Britain and these can be seen as the forerunners of the varieties now available. The wild apple trees have thorns: perhaps it was this that gave the apple its dangerous reputation.

Since the days of the old apple, growers have been busy improving the qualities of existing varieties and developing new ones. This has led to a situation where virtually no apple trees are grown in their original form. The cultivated varieties now being grown cannot be propagated from seed and rooting cuttings takes too long.

A 'host stem' is now used, some other stem with roots, and a small branch from the particular fruit tree is grafted on to this. Apart from providing swift propagation, this also gives the advantage of being able to control the shape and strenght of the tree. Host stems have their own advantages and disadvantages, so alongside the cultivation of apples, there has developed a separate science on the cultivation of these host stems. Of course, none of this is as important for the gardener as it is for the commercial grower. Even so, you have a choice from the varieties that remain small and those that grow tall, and you should be aware of the consequences attendant upon that choice. The tall, broad trees are more attractive, but they take longer to bear fruit, are more difficult to care for, and take up a lot of space. Despite these disadvantages, the interest in these 'traditional' apple trees is reviving and they are again easily available. But, as we said, the newer types are more practical, particularly when you remember that just about every variety needs to be cross-pollinated. This means that you need two different types of apple tree planted close together in order to get good fruit. For example, the early ripening Discovery needs Cox or Benoni for cross-pollination. For the famous Golden Delicious you will need a Cox or James Grieve. This latter apple ripens rather late (first half of September), whilst Golden Delicious is a good storage apple, as is Golden Renet. The sweet apples (e.g. Dijkmans sweet and Sweet Ermgaard) are self-pollinating, so these can be planted alone. There are therefore many possibilities.

An apple tree makes few demands on the soil. Fertilise it each March or April and prune it back into shape in January. However, if you want the tree to stay small, then prune it as little as possible because pruning promotes the growth. In essence, the apple is an easy fruit tree to grow even though you should not expect the same results as the professional grower.

MORUS nigra
Black Mulberry

Flowering period: insignificant.
Colour: pink(blossom), purplish red(fruit).
Height: 3-6 metres in 10-15 years.
The mulberry is virtually an antique tree. As well as having useful fruit, it is also very attractive. Particularly nice is the Morus alba 'Pendula' with its drooping shape. The fruit, deep purple when fully mature, often falls from the tree before it is properly ripe: but it can still be used for jam or drinks. It needs a sheltered, sunny spot and lime rich soil. In Asia, its leaves are used as food for silkworms.

PRUNUS avium
Wild Cherry

Flowering period: April to May.
Colour: white(blossom), yellow to red(autumn leaf).
Height: 15-20 metres.
Most of the trees that bear eating cherries come from the Prunus avium. However, it is often found growing as an ornamental cherry, even when the dark red cherries are edible. It prefers a not too heavy, lime rich, well drained soil in the full sun. Its wood is used for making furniture and instruments. But in general it is found adorning gardens, parks and streets.

PRUNUS cerasus
Sour Cherry

Flowering period: March to April.
Colour: pale pink(blossom), pale red(fruit).
Height: 1.5 to 5 metres.
The fruit of the Prunus cerasus is too sour to be eaten raw, but is very good for making jam. The best known is the Morello, an old variety the origin of which has been forgotten. There is a miniature variety of the Morello available that grows no taller than 1.5 metres. The sour cherry grows best in lime rich, fertile soil. The fruit forms on the one year old wood, so it should be pruned annually in September; young trees less than older ones.

PRUNUS domestica
Plum

Flowering period: April.
Colour: pale pink(blossom), yellow, blue, green and red(fruit).
Height: 2-5 metres.
The plum comes originally from the Caucasus but is now grown throughout Europe. Like most apples, pears and cherries, the plum is dependent on cross pollination, although some such as Victoria, Czar and Opal are self-pollinating. Its needs lime rich, fertile, moist soil and a sunny, sheltered spot. After the fruit is picked, prune the longer branches to keep it in shape.

PYRUS communis 'Conference'
Pear

Flowering period: May.
Colour: white(blossom).
Height: 3-5 metres.
With so many exotic fruits available these days, the apple and pear seem to be very British. They are fruit trees that make few demands on climate or soil (but this must not be too rich in lime).
Pears grown commercially are grafted onto a host stem. These small trees bear fruit much quicker, and can be kept small since they are grown only for their fruit. In the garden, however, the fruit is less important than whether you want a large or small pear tree.

PYRUS communis 'Doyenné du Comice'
Pear

Flowering period: May.
Colour: White(blossom).
Height: 3-5 metres.
With a little care the pear tree will provide excellent fruit in our climate. The tree must be protected against diseases and the fruit from birds and wasps. Although its blossom is lovely, the tree is not very attractive; it is the fruit that makes it worth growing. It needs to be cross pollinated, so two varieties should be planted. A well known combination is Doyenne du Comice and Conference (described previously). Comice has a strong smell and is very juicy.

RIBES 'Red Rebel'
Red currant

Flowering period: April.
Colour: pale green(flower).
Height: 1-2 metres.
'Red Rebel' is one of the newest of the red currants, of which there are countless varieties varying in size and quality. However, for a small garden these differences are of little interest. The currant is planted in sandy soil, as a shrub or to form a hedge – in a row supported by wire (see illustration). To ensure good fruit, treat the plant annually with a fair amount of organic fertiliser and prune it so that it gets sufficient air.

RIBES nigrum
Black currant

Flowering period: April.
Colour: green-white(flower), black(fruit).
Height: 1 to 1.5 metres.
Even those who have never actually seen a blackcurrant will recognise the flavour. It is really only grown for the production of blackcurrant juice or jam, because the flavour of the fresh currants is not very pleasant. Unlike the previous two, this one is not suitable for a hedge but should be planted alone. The currants form in largest numbers on the new wood, so the shrub should be well pruned each year. Light, fertile, moist soil.

PRUNUS

The Prunus has already received extra attention under shrubs because there are so many different varieties. It also features prominently in the fruit section because cherry, plum, apricot, peach, almond and morello all belong to the Prunus family. But even though they are often so different, they do have one thing in common: they carry fruit with usually just one seed, the stone. With the fruit bearing Prunus it is the juicy flesh around the stone that is eaten – except with the almond, where the pip itself is the fruit. There is another exceptional thing about the almond: it is the only Prunus that does not ripen well in our climate. Of course, it is not easy to grow the apricot or peach in Britain, but it is not impossible. However, grown outdoors the almond will not give the soft pips that are harvested in late September in the Mediterranean countries. Even so, the almond (Prunus dulcis) is worth growing. In March or April the beautiful deep pink blossom unfurls, inspiration of many poets. In fertile, lime rich soil it will grow into a fair size tree with wide spread branches. It is important to prune the branches right back once a year because the new buds form on the young shoots. It should come as no surprise that the almond must have a spot as sunny and sheltered as possible.

In many ways the same goes for the peach (Prunus persica) and the apricot (Prunus armenicaca). Because of night frosts, it is very unlikely that you will obtain good fruit if it is grown outdoors in our climate. However, you can grow a variety that remains small, like Prunus armenicaca 'Pêche de Nancy', in a large tub indoors until it flowers. Then, still in its tub, put it outside once there is no more likelihood of night frosts. The chance of good fruit is then considerably greater. The instructions for the almond also apply to the peach and apricot.

Sweet and sour cherries (Prunus avium and Prunus cerasus), do extremely well in our climate but they are not so often grown these days because there is no suitable host stem for the cherry as there is for the apple. A popular cherry is the Meikers, a hybrid of sweet and sour, that has the advantage of being self-pollinating, unlike the sweet cherry. The best known sour cherry, the Morello, cannot be eaten raw but can certainly be used for making jam and kirsch.

The Prunus domestica or plum is often grown in Britain and the fruit can be blue, red, yellow or green in colour. The greatest threat to the fruit is from night frosts. Otherwise, the plum is happy with lime rich, fertile soil and a sunny, sheltered spot. After the fruit is picked, prune it slightly to encourage a good crown.

RIBES uva-crispa
Gooseberry

Flowering period: April.
Colour: yellow(flower), yellow-green or purple(fruit).
Height: 1 to 1.5 metres.
Of all the Ribes the gooseberry is one of the least popular: because of the hours needed for picking; and also perhaps because of its distinctive flavour which is less popular than it used to be. However, the gooseberry makes delicious jam. It can be planted free standing or supported by wire, in moist, well drained and slightly lime rich soil. Prune away the old wood after the fruit.

ROSA canina
Dog Rose

Flowering period: June.
Colour: pale pink(blossom), red(fruit).
Height: 2.5 to 3.5 metres.
When the flowers are left on rose bushes, they later form fruit: the rose hip. On some of the wild or dog roses this fruit is edible and can be made into jams or jellies. Like the berry of the Sea Buckthorn, the rose hip is rich in vitamin C. The dog rose is a tall bush that makes few demands on the soil and needs little attention. To prevent it from running wild, it should be pruned in February. Its upright and sturdy growth makes it a good hedge.

ROSA rugosa
Rose

Flowering period: May to September.
Colour: purple-red(flower), orange(fruit).
Height: 1.5 to 2 metres.
This is a rose from East Asia. It is a broad, bushy shrub with lovely flowers measuring 9 cm.
As it grows in the poorest of sandy soils and withstands salty air, it is often found growing in dunes. In a garden it makes a particularly nice hedge. The large hips can be used in making jam or jelly. It needs full sun to fully ripen the fruit. After its long flowering period, the leaves turn golden yellow in autumn

RUBUS fruticosus
Blackberry

Flowering period: May.
Colour: white(blossom), blue-black(fruit).
Height: up to 1 metre, by a width of 3-4 m.
The Rubus fruticosus is a bramble that grows wild in woods and along hedgerows. The branches are covered with small thorns that fasten themselves over and around other plants with immense strength. It is therefore a good creeper and will thrive in places where nothing else will grow. It requires very little attention other than an annual prune in late autumn, and makes no demands on soil or surroundings.

RUBUS 'Thornless Evergreen'
Blackberry

Flowering period: May.
Colour: white(blossom), blue-black(fruit).
Height: up to 1 metre, by a width of 3-4 m.
Our last Rubus is another cultivated variety, with a very pleasant feature. This blackberry from America has no thorns, which makes care of the plant and picking of the fruit a lot easier.
Its fruit is also much prettier than that of the wild bramble. So, there are many good reasons for choosing this thornless bramble over the wild one. It is usually found growing as a hedge or along a wall or balcony.

RUBUS idaeus
Raspberry

Flowering period: May.
Colour: white(flower), red, white, black(fruit).
Height: up to 1 metre, by 3 metres(creeper).
Unlike the sturdy blackberry with its sharp thorns, the raspberry has more gentle prickles, and is altogether softer as a plant and as a fruit. In fact, so soft is it that it is a good idea to support it with wire. It needs well drained, humus rich soil and a sunny spot. There are early and late raspberries: the late (autumn) raspberry does not bloom until August and the red, white or black fruit is ripe by Ocotober as long as the weather is favourable.

RUBUS loganbaccus
Loganberry

Flowering period: May to June.
Colour: pale pink(blossom), red(fruit).
Height: up to 1 metre.
The loganberry takes its name from the Californian grower Logan who obtained it by crossing the blackberry and raspberry. It looks and behaves much like the bramble. The fruit is a bit sharp but is worth making into jam and drinks. Like the bramble, it grows in all soils.
For the fullest fruit it must have sun. After the fruit, cut it right back which will improve its yield.

RUBUS phoenicolasius
Wineberry

Flowering period: June to July.
Colour: white, pale pink(blossom),orange-red(fruit).
Height: up to 3 metres.
The most striking thing about this Japanese shrub is the russet hairs that cover its branches. Otherwise, it differs little in appearance from the blackberry, except that its fruit is orange-red and sticky with a sharp taste. What it does have in common with the blackberry is that it will grow and bloom just about anywhere.

SAMBUCUS nigra
Elder

Flowering period: June to July.
Colour: white(flower), dark blue(fruit).
Height: up to 7 metres.
The elder grows wild from Europe to Siberia. Because it is a very sturdy tree, almost as persistent as a weed, it grows anywhere; but if you want it to bloom as fully as possible, plant it in fertile soil with lime. The flowers can be used for brewing tea, and the berries for making syrup, jam and wine. In fact, the berries are medicinal and help to prevent constipation, heart disease and influenza. Prune in spring.

VACCINIUM corymbosum
Blueberry

Flowering period: April.
Colour: pale pink(blossom), silver-blue(fruit).
Height: up to 2 metres.
This vaccinium and the other ones all belong to the family of heath plants; the Ericaceae. They are all shrubs that remain fairly low, even though the blueberry can reach 2 metres. Their leaves are leathery and turn a lovely colour in autumn before falling. This one only grows in peaty soil which must be kept moist. The berries form on the one year old wood so the bush should be pruned in Nov-Dec.

VACCINIUM myrtillus
Woodberry

Flowering period: April.
Colour: green-pink(blossom).
Height: up to 50 cm.
As with the previously described blueberry, this one also grows in light shade. It is generally found growing beneath shrubs and trees in woods. And like the blueberry it needs moist, acid soil; although this can be less so. It needs very little attention. As well as the common woodberry there is also the redberry, the fruit of which is used for making sauce for game and fowl.

VITIS vinifera
Grape (white)

Flowering period: May to June.
Colour: green-white(flower), white-green(fruit).
Height: up to several metres(climber).
Witte van der Laan and Seedling (both white), Boskoops Glory and Rembrandt (both blue) are all suitable for outdoor cultivation. If you buy a rooted cutting, first dig a large hole. Fill this with compost and several buckets of water.
Continue to water well during the first weeks.
A couple of times a year fertilise with mixed manure. As the grapes begin to form, thin out the bunches. Your first harvest can be expected in the second year. Good luck!

CHAPTER 5
HEDGES

A hedge can have many functions. First of all, it can be used to divide up the terrain. In view of the fact that this is usually just symbolic (otherwise there would be a tall fence), it makes little difference what sort of hedge is used. It can be small or large, wide or narrow, flowering or non-flowering. In all these cases, the marking out of the area is obvious.

However, things are different if you want the hedge as a windbreak. It is then important to choose a tall, thick hedge that retains its leaves. For this sort of hedge there are the traditional hedge plants like Ligustrum ovalifolium (privet), Baxus sempervirens (palm) and Taxus baccata (yew). The privet is cheap and grows quickly, whilst the yew, a conifer, is fairly expensive and grows slowly.

You should consider these differences when buying, because they are important in the planting of your hedge! If you also want the hedge for privacy, then the same considerations apply.

However, if you would like the hedge to be the background to your garden, then you can choose either a restful, ever-green hedge or a colourful flowering one. Examples of the flowering hedge are on pages 88 and 89.

To lay a hedge you will need to dig a long trench in which to plant the young trees or shrubs at the correct distance apart. Once planted, water them well for the first few weeks until they are well established. Shortly after planting, prune the little plants well back to encourage a broader base. When clipping (for most types twice a year in June and August) leave the underneath a bit wider than the top so that it gets sufficient sun. Obviously conifers are not pruned and the clipping is limited to some tidying up until the trees are too large. As a hedge plant, conifers are both a nuisance and very pretty.

BERBERIS frikartii 'Amstelveen'
Barberry

Flowering period: May to June.
Colour: yellow(flower), green(leaf).
Height: 50-80 cm.
The cultivated berberis 'Amstelveen' is an evergreen shrub found in many parks because it is particularly sturdy. It needs a somewhat acid soil but otherwise makes few demands on the soil or the surroundings – it grows just as well in the town or along the roadside as it does in the wild. Because of the dense foliage, this shrub is also used for hedges. It can be propagated in the summer from cuttings.

BUXUS sempervirens
Palm Tree

Flowering period: insignificant.
Colour: dark green(leaf).
Height: 3-6 metres.
The palm is ideal as a hedge plant because it can be easily shaped. Castle grounds often have decorative palm hedges into which animals, people and archways have been trimmed. Branches from the palm are used by Catholics to celebrate Palm Sunday. It is an evergreen that likes to stand in the full sun, although it will also grow in shade. It does best in peaty, moist soil. Left unpruned, it blooms with tiny yellow flowers.

CLEMATIS montana
Clematis

Flowering period: May to June.
Colour: pink.
Height: 2-3 metres(climber).
You will not often find the clematis as a hedge plant, but during its flowering period it is very pretty. The Clematis montana has average size flowers, 5-6 cm across. As a hedge it needs a fence or other support up which to climb, and you could have a 3 metres high hedge. The clematis prefers lime rich, loamy soil that holds its moisture. After it has bloomed, prune it well back. It loves sun, but the foot of the plant must be kept in shade.

CORNUS alba 'Elegantissima'
Dogwood

Flowering period: insignificant.
Colour: green with silver edge(leaf).
Height: up to 250 cm.
The Cornus shows to great advantage when several are planted close together, making it suitable for a hedge. It looks fresh in summer with its silver edged leaves, and colourful in winter with its red branches. It grows just as well in dry or moist soil and prefers to stand in the sun, unlike most other plants of its type. Prune well late March; this encourages a thick growth and prevents bare patches.

EUONYMUS fortunei 'Vegetus'
Cardinal's hat

Flowering period: May.
Colour: green-yellow(flower), white(fruit).
Height: 1-2 metres.
This is an evergreen cardinal's hat, which is of particular advantage for a hedge. It makes no special demands on the soil and copes equally well with sun or shade. The leaf is thick, oval and leathery. When ripe, the white fruit bursts open displaying bright orange seeds. Prune slightly in autumn or spring. Like Euonymus planipes, this one comes from the mountains of Japan.

FAGUS sylvatica
Beech

Flowering period: insignificant.
Colour: green or russet(leaf).
Height: up to 30 metres.
The beech forms a thick, impenetrable hedge even in winter, because the old leaves remain on the shrub until the new ones open. Most of them make nice hedges as they are easy to prune and shape.
Use young trees, about 1 metre tall, for the basis of the hedge, and plant them at least 40 cm apart. The height of the hedge is then determined by pruning. Beech prefers loamy soil, but will grow in just about any type of earth.

FORSYTHIA
Forsythia

Flowering period: April.
Colour: yellow(flower).
Height: 2.5 to 3 metres.
The forsythia is not the first plant that springs to mind for a hedge, but it forms a summer green wall that blooms richly with tiny yellow flowers in early spring, when there are few other flowers on show. If you prune it well each year, you will have a reasonably thick hedge in summer; in winter it is a bit bare. Forsythia needs well drained, fertile soil with lime.

HYPERICUM patulum
St. John's Wort

Flowering period: July to August.
Colour: golden yellow(flower).
Height: up to 1.5 metres.
With its pretty flowers, this Hypericum forms a very nice hedge. If the shrub is not pruned it grows rahter bushy, but is is easily trimmed into shape, preferably in spring before it blooms. The leathery leaves do tend to fall after a while, but the shrub retains some leaves virtually all year. This variety of Hypericum loves a spot in the full sun, but makes no other special demands on soil or surroundings.

FLOWERING HEDGES

A hedge is generally used for marking out a piece of
ground, for creating privacy, for protection against
the wind or for a combination of all three. But
sometimes these considerations are less important,
and the hedge is wanted mainly as a background for
the garden. In this case, it is worth thinking twice
before you choose a traditional hedge of privet, yew
or thuja. These have a dense growth and can be
trimmed into any shape you like, but with their hard
greenness they add very little to the appearance of a
garden. On the other hand, there are many shrubs
which lend themselves to use as a hedge and that,
with their lovely flowers, decorate your garden all
summer long. A good example is the Potentilla
fruticosa. This shrub grows about 1 metre high and
about the same in width, is fairly thick and blooms
from June to September or even October. The most
common varieties have yellow flowers, but there are
also cultivated types with white or red flowers.
It makes virtually no demands on the soil but must
have sun. As a hedge, it provides a flowery background to your garden all summer. Another
exuberant bloomer, not for so long but just as jolly,
is the Spiraea, which is very suitable as a hedge
because of its dense growth and height (up to 2
metres). Spiraea has white or red flowers and
blooms, depending on type, from April or May to
September. Particularly suitable are Spiraea arguta,
which blooms in spring with masses of tiny white
flowers, and Spiraea bumalda 'Anthony Waterer', that
blooms from July to September with red flowers. An
obvious suggestion is to combine these two so that
you have a small, red flowering hedge in front of a
taller white one. The Spiraea is just as easy to grow
as Potentilla, but it is good for the shrub to prune out
the older branches after flowering.
Another suggestion for a flowering hedge is
Symphoricarpos. Not only does it flower the whole
summer, but it also bears red or white berries until
well into winter. In addition, it has the advantage that
it grows quite well in shade. None of these three
needs very much attention. But if you want to invest

some time in a flowering hedge, try the Azalea. The
disadvantage is that it does not bloom for long, but
the flowers are particularly pretty. You will find some
information on how to look after an Azalea hedge in
the description of this shrub on page 16.
Aside from these four suggestions, there are many
other possibilities and a few of these are covered in
this chapter. It is well worth bearing in mind when
choosing your hedge plant that you can use it to give
extra colour to your garden.

LIGUSTRUM ovalifolium
Privet

Flowering period: July.
Colour: white(flower), black(berry), green(leaf).
Height: up to 5 metres.
Many people are unaware that this shrub has flowers because it is generally trimmed before it can bloom. Privet is predominantly used as a hedge; trimmed three times a year to form a neat barrier that ensures privacy. It makes absolutely no demands and remains partly green, although it is not completely winter resistant; in fact, if the frost attacks it, it is better to cut it right back to its base.

PRUNUS cistena
Flowering Cherry

Flowering period: April to May.
Colour: pal pink(blossom), dark red(leaf).
Height: 1-2 metres.
The family of Prunus contains hundreds of trees and shrubs that vary considerably in shape and flower: from drooping to ball shaped; from white to red blossoms; from dwarf bush to tree; from fruit tree to ornamental shrub; all occur in this family. Like most Prunus, this one needs chalky, well drained soil and full sun. It is sturdy, and its dense growth and beautiful blossom turn a hedge into a wall of colour.

TAXUS baccata
Yew

Flowering period: insignificant.
Colour: red(fruit).
Height: 3-10 metres.
The fruit of the yew is very tasty but unfortunately the seeds in the fruit are poisonous, as are its needles. Like the palm, a hedge of yews can be trimmed into any shape. It is an evergreen that makes few demands, except that the soil must be well drained. It is very sturdy and can grow to a great age: around the Walchen Sea in West Germany there are 1000 year old yew trees.

THUJA occidentalis 'Little Champion'
Cedar

Flowering period: insiginificant.
Colour: green(needles).
Height: up to 80 cm.
There is really just one thing necessary for growing the cedar, and that is well drained soil.
Like most other conifers, it is an evergreen.
Because of its dense foliage it is often used as a hedge. Although this is not the case with the one shown here, which is a swarf. It is a very round shrub, generally planted alone or between other low plants. It looks particularly nice in a heather garden.

INDEX SHADE-LOVING SHRUBS

Nearly all plants need sunlight for growing and flowering. Yet there are some shrubs that prefer shade, under bushes or on a spot in your garden where the sun does not reach.

The plants mentioned below are of this type, and you will find that with these plants you can even make a garden facing north something beautiful!

Azalea (evergreen)
(**B**uddleia)
Cardinals Hat
(Cherry)
(Cotoneaster)
(**D**ogwood)
Elder
Fir
Hazel
Honeysuckle
Hydrangca
Ivy
Jasmine
Juniper
Mahonia
Palm Tree
Prickly Heath
Privet
Rhododendron
Rubus (various berries)
(**S**hrubby Cinquefoil)
Skimmia
Snowberry
St. John's Wort
(**V**iburnum)
Woodberry
Yew

GROUND-COVERING SHRUBS

(**B**arberry)
Broom
(**C**ardinals Hat)
(Cotoneaster)
(**D**ogwood)
Heath
Ivy
(**J**uniper)
Lesser Periwinkle
Prickley Heath
Rubus (various berries)
(**S**nowberry)
(Spiraea)
St. John's Wort
(**V**iburnum)
(**Y**ew)

CLIMBERS

Clematis
Grape
Honeysuckle
(Hydrangea)
Ivy
Knottgrass
Passion Flower
Pyracanthus
Rubus (various berries)
Trumpet Vine
Vine
Wisteria

EVERGREEN SHRUBS

Andromeda
(Barberry)
Blueberry
Cardinals Hat
(Cherry)
(Cotoneaster)
Heath
Holly
Ivy

Lesser Periwinkle
Mahonia
Palm Tree
Prickley Heath
Privet
Pyracanthus
(Rhododendron)
Skimmia
St. John's Wort

ORNAMENTAL FRUIT

Barberry
Beauty Berry
(Cardinals Hat)
(Cherry)
Cotoneaster
Dwarf Quince
Elder
Hawthorn
Holly
(Honeysuckle)
Mahonia

Mountain Ash
Passion Flower
(Pepper Tree)
Prickley Heath
Pyracanthus
Rose
Sea Buckthorn
Skimmia
Snowberry
(Viburnum)

AROMATIC FLOWERS OR FOLIAGE

Apple
Blue Spiraea
Broom
Buddleia
Cedar
Cherry
Dwarf Quince
Fir
Flowering Currant
Hawthorn

Honeysuckle
Jasmine
Pepper Tree
Rose
Skimmia
Spiraea
Syringa
(Viburnum)
Yew

N.B. The plantnames bracketed refer to plants of which not all varieties show the property in question.

INDEX OF PLANT NAMES

INDEX OF PLANT NAMES

INDEX OF PLANT NAMES

NOTES

NOTES